MW01154120

KILL YOUR CARDS

Please Read This FIRST

Terms of Use

The Kill Your Cards book is Copyright © 2012. All rights reserved. No part of this book may be reproduced, stored in a retrieval system, or transmitted by any means; electronic, mechanical, photo copying, recording or otherwise, without written permission from the copyright holders. You do not have any right to distribute any part of this paperback book or electronic book in any way at all. T. Swike and indyebooks are the sole distributors. Violators will be prosecuted.

The contents of this book are intended for entertainment only. The opinions contained in this book are NOT legal advice, and should not be interpreted as legal advice, or council. Always consult the services of an attorney whenever you need legal advice. USE AT YOUR OWN RISK.

Several trademarks are used in this book for narrative purposes. Each trademark is the property of its respective owners.

Copyright 2012

ISBN-10: 1470150565
ISBN-13: 978-1470150563

TABLE OF CONTENTS

INTRODUCTION

So here you are, mired in credit card debt. How did this happen? More importantly, how will you pay all these bills with their escalating interest rates? And if you really want to lose sleep at night, consider what the future holds – endless calls from collection agencies, a destroyed credit rating, and maybe even bankruptcy.

You could really beat yourself up about this, but don't. You did nothing wrong. That's right. YOU are not to blame! This is how the credit card game is played; only no one told you the rules.

The simple truth is, the credit card system is so stacked against you that you CAN'T win. Unless you pay off your credit card balance immediately after each purchase, with each swipe of your card, you're falling deeper and deeper into credit card hell.

Credit card companies have only one goal, which is to make as much money as possible before the gig is up. The politically incorrect term for this behavior is GREED. Why else would they raise interest rates on once-loyal customers falling behind on their payments?

Welcome to the credit card game, one of the most brilliant scams of our time, where credit card companies have somehow managed to make the financial ruin of their customers not only legal, but prosperous. Through outrageously high interest rates, annual fees, usage fees, over- the- limit fees, late fees and penalties, credit card companies have positioned themselves to take all your money. Remember, there are no morals in this credit card game, just winners and losers. They want to take all of your money, and you want to hold on to all of your money. They will do anything to get your money, and you need to be able to do anything to keep your money. It's time to learn how the banks play.

One way the banks try to grab your money is by changing your interest rate. Did you know it's completely legal for a credit card company to charge an interest rate of 79.9%? Don't believe me? Google "First Premiere Bank Card 79.9%" and see what some of their customers are paying. And boy do they have fees, too. Wonder how many of them will default? And when they default, and millions of other people default due to the shaky economy, will the banks get another huge taxpayer-funded bailout? You bet they will, and then it will be business as usual. But this time, you won't be their victim!

In this book, you'll learn about some credit card laws that are on YOUR side. And you'll get tips on how to respond to the harassment and fear tactics that credit card companies and collection agencies use to drain your funds. Knowledge is power, so soak it up, pass it on, and get ready to rid your life of credit card debt and misery!

So let's get started. This book describes 6 simple steps for beating the credit card and collection companies. These steps are techniques that I have used to settle thousands of dollars worth of debt for 20 cents on the dollar. And you can do this, too. Especially now, when the economy is in a horrible recession, and people are not paying their bills. They are sick of spending all of their income on gas, insurance, and food. All of which have gone up in price due to inflation and greed. And this trend will continue to go on as long as the Federal Reserve keeps printing out money to pay for our country's wars and debts. So as the dollar continues to decline in value, inflation rises, and the cost of goods goes up. Inflation is the worst tax there is because it really beats up the poor and middle class. The end result is what we have now, a negative savings economy. When you factor in the amount spent on credit cards, people are actually spending more money than they make in a year. This type of lifestyle was unheard of several decades ago. People had savings back then and a higher standard of living. Nowadays, people have little if any money in savings and loads of debt.

This debt based system is designed to keep us slaves to the big central banks. And it is working. Have you ever used a credit card to pay for rent or even another credit card bill? Or, have you sold items on Ebay, just to pay credit card bills? Then you know what I'm talking about. In fact, your own government does this same exact thing. Why? Because there is not enough money in circulation to pay for all of its debts. Each time private central banks like the Federal Reserve print off money, they are basically giving out a loan plus interest that our government has to pay back. So more money has to be loaned out to pay for the previous loan plus interest. That's exactly what happens when you adopt a debt based currency provided by private central banks, which is what happened under the Federal Reserve Act of 1913. Here is how it works. Let's say a new government needs money, $1 billion to be exact. Since only the Federal Reserve can print out and regulate the value of this money, the new government must sell $1 billion worth of treasury bonds, or IOU's, in exchange for the newly created money (Federal Reserve Notes), which is also worth $1 billion. The bonds act as security for the new loan. Interest is owed on this newly printed money, which means this loan can never be fully paid off. $1 billion dollars plus interest is owed, but there is only $1 billion dollars in circulation. This means the new government will always be in debt to the bankers no matter how much money they create. And if the bankers can control the debt of a nation, they can control everything. They can control the politicians, foreign policy, and your livelihood. Remember, the Federal Reserve is a private corporation. And corporations do what makes them the most money, regardless of who gets hurt. Don't believe me? Just take a look at every war our country entered since 1913, or take a look at every economic recession, depression, bailout, or inflationary period our country has had to endure. The Federal Reserve has profited from our country's hardships time and time again. They will do anything in their power to force the government to borrow more money.

There is, however, a small but significant silver lining to this story. The good news is the credit card companies and banks are now feeling some of this pain, too. People just don't have the money to pay their bills anymore. And the banks are now having to write off billions of dollars of unpaid debt. This ultimately means better deals for you and me. Just take a look at HSBC, for example. They had to get out of the store branded credit card game in the USA because it was no longer profitable due to the poor economic conditions here. They sold the loans for around $32.7 billion to Capital One, while cutting thousands of jobs. Credit card companies can't sue everyone, so they have to make deals with the consumer if they want to get paid.

On that note, let's move on to step 1.

Check out The Raw Story to read more about HSBC. http://www.rawstory.com/rs/2011/08/09/hsbc-to-sell-credit-card-business/

HSBC to sell credit card business

By Agence France-Presse
Tuesday, August 9th, 2011 -- 7:53 am

HSBC said Tuesday it is in talks to sell its United States credit card and retail services business as the global banking giant shifts focus to fast-growing markets, particularly in Asia.

The lender has unveiled massive cost-cutting measures in recent months, including plans to save up to $3.5 billion by 2013 and to axe 30,000 jobs across the globe over the next two years.

But the bank has also said it will hire up to 15,000 people in emerging markets by 2014 as it looks to Asia's booming financial sector to power future growth.

Tags: credit card loans, dow jones newswires, first niagara bank

"HSBC confirms that it is in discussions regarding a possible sale of the business," the bank said in a statement issued through its Hong Kong office.

STEP 1 – STOP PAYING YOUR BILLS

The first step is probably the easiest, yet one of the most important. It involves stopping payment on all of your credit cards. Remember, your credit cards are unsecured debt. They do not involve any collateral that can be repossessed. Plus, it is not illegal to refuse to pay your credit cards. In other words, you can't go to jail unless the laws change. So you will need to stop paying on most, if not all of you cards. This step is essential for convincing the credit card companies of a few things:

1. You have no money. The more money you have, the less chance there is that the credit companies will be willing to make a deal. If they think you have the money, your negotiating powers are all gone. Make them think you are broke instead. When they call you up and ask why you haven't made a payment in a while, simply tell them "loss of income, due to recession." Or say "lost job." Anything else is none of their business. You don't need credit counseling from some loser that makes collection calls all day for minimum wage. So don't take any. Often, these people are poor and uneducated, yet they still try to intimidate you into paying your bills by passing judgment.

So when you do talk to them, remember, everything you say will be used against you. That's why they record everything. It's none of their business where the money will come from to make a settlement. As far as they are concerned, your income is $0. Don't give them a reason to think otherwise. Keep in mind, if you make payments on other cards, it will show up on your credit report, and the card companies will see that you are paying some bills. Continue to pay your secured debt, like your car or mortgage payment. But stop paying your credit cards all at once. This will look like you got hit hard by unemployment, or some type of major medical bill. Since the average consumer has around 7 credit cards and $18,000 worth of debt, it's easy to see how one can get lost in debt with just a few late payments, resulting in 30% interest on that $18,000. Your debt is now too big to pay down!

2. You have no job, or steady income stream. Don't ever tell the credit card companies that you have a good job. Tell them instead you were laid off or fired, or your work hours were cut back. No job, no money= less likely to get sued. Plus, it is none of their business! Just like their terms and conditions change every few months, so have yours. One credit card company once asked me to get another job so I could pay my bills. If this happens to you, tell them "you are not a credit counselor, so mind your own damn business."

3. You don't care about your credit score. The credit card companies love to use this threat all the time. Your credit rating will be lowered and your bills will be written off as bad debt and reported to the credit bureaus. So what? You can fight that, too, when the time is right. When a company writes off a bad debt or "charge off", it's just a tax write off term for the IRS. It's a loss of income that they don't have to pay taxes on. The good news is that charge offs also mean an end to the outrageous fees and interest being charged each month. And that is usually the time when they consider assigning or selling your debt to a third party. This means that the debt has just decreased in value! Tell them to go ahead and charge it off today! Get the ball rolling.

4. You have no assets. A credit card counseling company once asked me if I had furniture to sell to pay for my debts. I laughed and soon realized these places were a waste of my time. I would much rather keep my furniture and not pay the credit card companies. That would have been some useful advice! The point here is don't tell the credit card companies that you have anything of value. Don't admit to owning anything they don't know about. They can see if you are listed on a mortgage or car payment. But, if you don't have your name on a mortgage or car payment, then you are in a great position. The card companies will think that you can just disappear at any time, making them more willing to offer a settlement.

Step one will take about 4 months. Unfortunately, you will be getting annoying calls every day by the end of month one. You may want to turn off your ringer or call up your phone company to see how many phone numbers you can block. There is no real reason to talk with your creditors the first few months, since they won't be willing to make you a deal yet. You will just have to wait it out. You might have to block some of the calls on your phone. Often you can do that through your phone company's website. The link below shows AT&T's call blocking procedure. Note: do not block calls after 120 days.

http://www.att.com/gen/general?pid=3491

Or you can sign up for the AT&T Smart Limits for Wireless Plan, which lets you block 30 numbers for $5 a month. Odds are, your phone service can help you with this problem for the first 4 months.

http://www.att.net.net/smartcontrols-smartlimitsforwireless

Many other options exist for smart phones, like assigning a silent ringtone to the number you want to block. Check out this link for detailed instructions.

http://www.mylittleportal.com/call-block-cell-phone-number-iphone

If you have an Iphone, you can buy a cool application for $1.99 that will allow you to identify thousands of user submitted numbers assigned to bill collectors, so you know not to answer the phone.

http://itunes.apple.com/us/app/blacklist/id310726855?mt=8

Check out the National Do Not Call registry to block collection calls for free.

https://donotcall.gov/default.aspx

After several months have passed, you can start taking the calls, and the credit cards will realize that you, at the very least, are having real financial difficulty. When that time comes, you will be ready to look for a deal. If your credit card companies get you on the phone in the first few months. Just tell them you lost your job and will try to pay them as soon as possible. Then hang up. Don't waste your time. Remember, they won't offer you anything good at this point. Don't accept any hardship programs or lower interest programs. Those are often tricks that will keep you in debt even longer. You are just prolonging the inevitable by agreeing to give them ANY money, so don't. Save the money for settlements, not payments. Stick to your game plan. You don't have a job, money, or assets.

Google has plenty of information on blocking calls.

STEP 2 – DEALING WITH THE ORIGINAL CREDITOR

The 4-6 month period is when you need to start talking to the credit card companies and start asking them for a 20% settlement. Usually an account will be charged off at around the 180 day mark, so right before you hit 180 is when you will get offered the best deal by the original creditor. When the account "charges off" it means that a credit card company has changed the account from an "accounts receivable" status to a "bad debt" status. This prevents the sleezy banks from inflating future earnings. For the consumer, it just means that you get an R9 status on your credit report. You didn't pay your debt. Big deal. Your credit can be fixed, too. But we will worry about that later. The main thing is, when the credit card company calls and says your account will charge off, tell them to go ahead and do it. It's a weak threat, so don't let it intimidate you.

On the next page you will see a typical threatening letter that the credit companies will send off. This letter has two main threats. One is the "Written off as a Bad Debt" tactic, which means you have bad credit. You already knew that though. The other tactic is the threat of dealing with a collection agency. This letter leaves you to believe that collection agencies are not flexible, and hard to deal with. But the truth is, it is much harder for a collection agency to get at your money, unless they trick you. Plus, the debt also decreases in value after it is purchased by another company. The collection agencies are more willing to take a settlement offer, since it means they make an easy profit. For example, they bought the debt for 1-3 cents on the dollar, and are willing to take 10 cents on the dollar as a settlement. In this case, having the debt move to a collection agency is a good thing. And the older the debt it, the less money the debt will be worth, which means a better settlement or possibly no settlement at all. If no one can get at your money, all you have to do is wait for your state's Statute of Limitations to pass and you are debt free. Note: I am only talking about a collection agency that has legally purchased the debt for right now. Never give money to a collection agency that has been assigned the debt. They are just hired to make phone calls and cannot do anything to you legally. They cannot validate any debt you have. Never admit to owing a debt to anyone except the original creditor. Even if the collector that bought the debt offers you 10 cents on the dollar, and you want the deal. In that case, you could pay the collector to stop harassing you, but you would never admit to owing the debt. On the other hand, that same junk debt buyer or collection agency probably cannot prove that you actually owe the debt, so you might not have to pay the debt ever. Once the statute of limitations has run out, the debt is legally gone. And if you can get that debt buyer to sell to another debt buyer, then you are home free. The chances of proving the case against you in court are minimal at that point. Are you starting to see how the game is played?

Check out some of the offer letters from my original creditors on the next few pages.

Note: my address and credit card numbers have been blocked out of the images displayed in this book.

Cardmember Service
P.O. Box 15548
Wilmington, DE 19886-5548

Time Sensitive

February 23, 2011

Լ.Լ

Account Number Ending: ███   Outstanding balance: $1,737.45

Dear ████████

Your Account is Scheduled to Be Written off as a Bad Debt

Your credit card account is seriously past due. Payment of your amount due of $565.00 will avoid any additional collection activities. If you do not pay your bill immediately, we will write your account off as a bad debt to comply with regulatory guidelines. When your account is written off, we will also report this account as such to the credit reporting organizations. As a result, your credit rating could be severely impacted for years to come. This blemish on your credit report could seriously limit your eligibility for future loans and/or increase the interest rate you pay. This blemish may also limit your ability to rent a car, book a hotel room or buy a car.

You should also know that even after we write off your account, we may take the following actions:

1. We may continue to contact you to make payment. Even after your debt is written off, you're still responsible to pay the balance on your credit card account. We may continue to call you and demand payment on the outstanding credit card balance.

2. Your account may be sent to a debt collection agency or sold to a purchaser of bad debt who specializes in collections. These agencies specialize in the collection of bad debt and may contact you to make payment on your outstanding credit card balance. When your account is placed with an agency, you will no longer be able to take advantage of our flexible payment options.

It is our sincere hope that we can avoid these unpleasant alternatives. To bring your account up to date and out of collections, we need to receive a payment of $565.00 from you immediately. To keep your account from becoming past due, you must continue to make at least your minimum payment each month. If you have any questions, we encourage you to call a Customer Support Representative at 1-866-965-9305.

Sincerely,

Customer Support Division

Here is another "bad debt" letter from FIA. The notes show a 20% settlement that was about to be accepted.

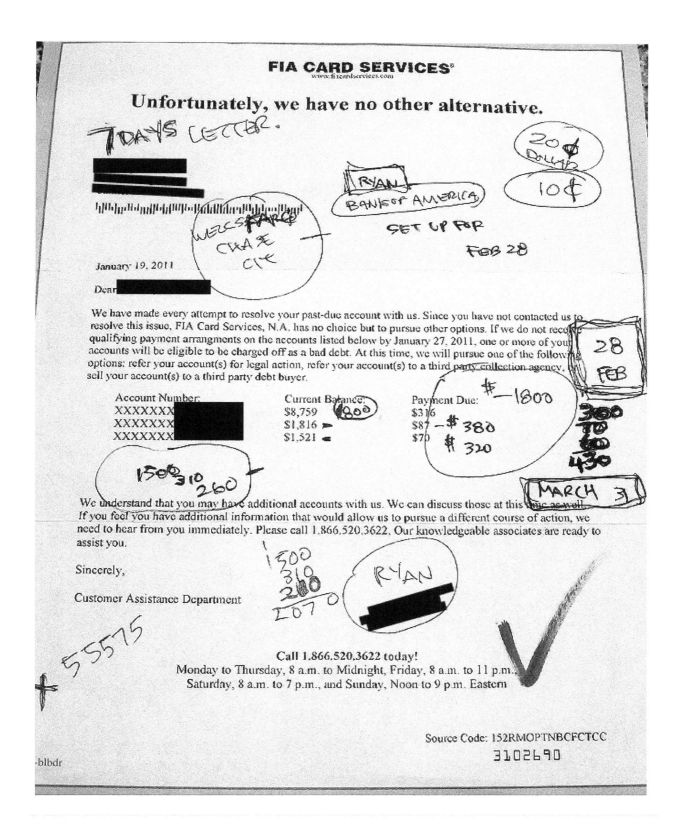

FIA CARD SERVICES®
www.fiacardservices.com

Unfortunately, we have no other alternative.

January 19, 2011

Dear

We have made every attempt to resolve your past-due account with us. Since you have not contacted us to resolve this issue, FIA Card Services, N.A. has no choice but to pursue other options. If we do not receive qualifying payment arrangements on the accounts listed below by January 27, 2011, one or more of your accounts will be eligible to be charged off as a bad debt. At this time, we will pursue one of the following options: refer your account(s) for legal action, refer your account(s) to a third party collection agency, or sell your account(s) to a third party debt buyer.

Account Number:	Current Balance:	Payment Due:
XXXXXXX	$8,759	$316
XXXXXXX	$1,816	$87
XXXXXXX	$1,521	$70

We understand that you may have additional accounts with us. We can discuss those at this time as well. If you feel you have additional information that would allow us to pursue a different course of action, we need to hear from you immediately. Please call 1.866.520.3622. Our knowledgeable associates are ready to assist you.

Sincerely,

Customer Assistance Department

Call 1.866.520.3622 today!
Monday to Thursday, 8 a.m. to Midnight, Friday, 8 a.m. to 11 p.m.
Saturday, 8 a.m. to 7 p.m., and Sunday, Noon to 9 p.m. Eastern

Source Code: 152RMOPTNBCFCTCC
3102690

-blbdr

Below is an example of a company ready to make a settlement after several months of non-payment. The deal you make, however, must be better than 55%. Never go over 30%. I like the pictures of barbells in the left column. Unfortunately, a 55% settlement does not take much weight off my shoulders.

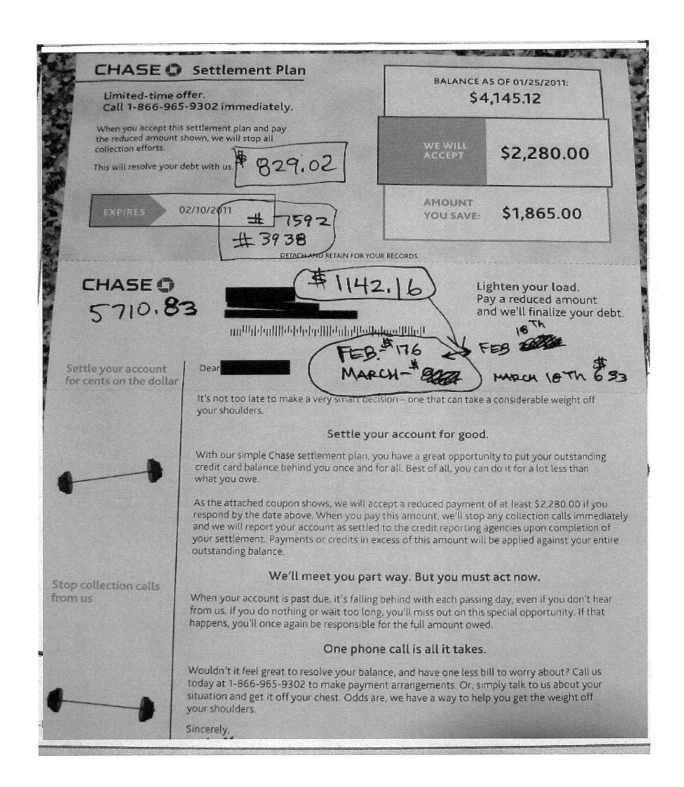

Here is an example of a letter you will receive after they refuse your first offer.

February 15, 2011

lldldlldllmdmdldddddddldbfddblldddddlddlldddddll

511 - NNNNNNNNNNNN

**Important information is
provided below regarding
your account.**

RE: Your account ending in 7592

Dear ▮▮▮▮▮▮

We have reviewed your request to settle your credit account. We appreciate the effort that you are making to pay down your outstanding balance. Unfortunately, we have determined that your account does not qualify for a settlement at this time.

We may have another payment option that is right for you. Please call us today at 1-888-792-7547.

Sincerely,

Customer Support Team

Account is owned by Chase Bank USA, N.A.

Let's get back to the phone calls. Here is how most, if not all of these calls original creditor will go. It will begin to sound like a broken record after a few weeks.

credit card company: *Hello is this Joe Smith?*

Joe: *Yes, it is.*

credit card company: *This is an attempt to collect a debt, and this call may be recorded for quality assurance. Now can i have the last 4 digits of your social security for identification?*

Joe: *9999 (Note: they already have this info.)*

credit card company: *Thanks. Can I get your address?*

Joe: *9999 Spring Dr., Chicago, IL, etc. (Note: they already have this info.)*

credit card company: *Thank you sir. I see that your account is 140 days past due with an outstanding balance of $2000. Can we set up a payment over the phone to get your account up to date?*

Joe: *No, thanks.*

credit card company: *(surprised) Why not?*

Joe: *Because of the recession. Loss of income. Lost my job.*

credit card company: *I'm sorry you are experiencing a hardship. Can we set you up with a payment program to bring your account up to date.*

Joe: *No, thanks.*

credit card company: *Joe. You need to bring your account up to date or else it will charge off and ruin your credit. How do you plan on settling your debt?*

Joe: *I would like a settlement for 20% in order to close out my account.*

credit card company: *(irritated) I'm sorry we can't do that. We do have a settlement program available for you for 60% of your debt. Can we set this up?*

Joe: *No, that won't work. Please call me back when you can do a 20% settlement. That's MY offer.*

credit card company: *Again I'm sorry you are having difficulty. What kind of work do you do?*

Joe: *I'm sorry, but I don't need any financial advice from you. I can only pay 20%. Call me back when you are ready to do that. Bye!*

Note: now is the time to see if a signed contract still exists, which can be used against you in court. You need to request this before the credit card company signs off the account to a collection agency. You need to know if it is still around. Often, the credit card company will give you an address to write to. Get the address and send them a request for a copy of the original signed contract. Often, creditors do not keep paperwork that is several years old. And that

includes the signed contracts or generic cardmember agreements. Now we can apply basic contract law to any potential lawsuit. No contract = no breach of contract.

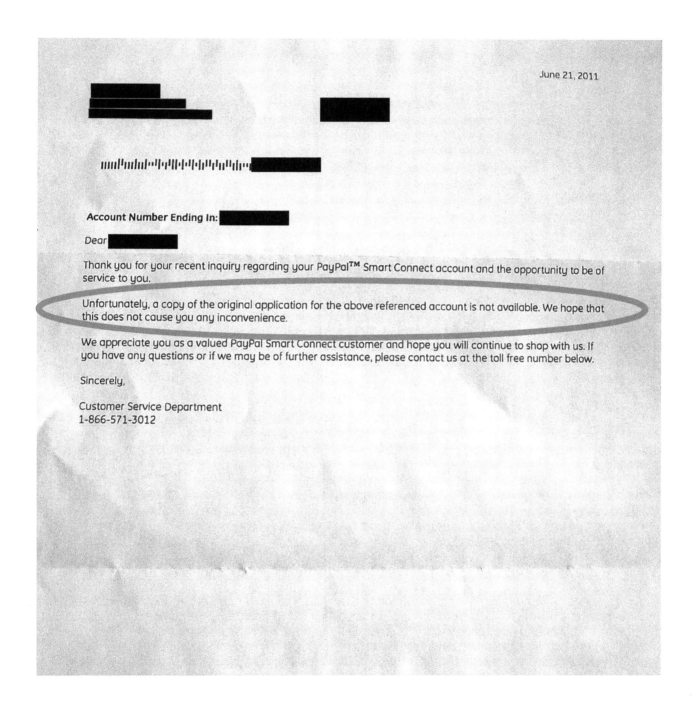

June 21, 2011

Account Number Ending In: ███████

Dear ███████

Thank you for your recent inquiry regarding your PayPal™ Smart Connect account and the opportunity to be of service to you.

Unfortunately, a copy of the original application for the above referenced account is not available. We hope that this does not cause you any inconvenience.

We appreciate you as a valued PayPal Smart Connect customer and hope you will continue to shop with us. If you have any questions or if we may be of further assistance, please contact us at the toll free number below.

Sincerely,

Customer Service Department
1-866-571-3012

Fast forward a few weeks. The offers usually get a little better. However, sometimes they don't. With Bank of America, I got them down to a 20% settlement on around $13,000 worth of debt. They were very easy to deal with. Other companies won't budge, and will often be rude on the phone. Here is a rude phone call:

credit card company: I'm sorry you are having financial problems, but you signed the contract with the credit card company. Don't you think you are responsible for paying off your debts? Now how are we going to resolve this?

Joe: I have paid the principle balance (what i actually charged) many times over. It's your ridiculous fees and interest rates that have made it impossible for me to pay my bills. I'm sorry but I didn't get a TARP bailout ($700 billion Troubled Asset Relief Program) to pay my bills like you did (Capital One, Bank of America, and Citigroup are examples). And I never agreed to pay 30% in interest. Please send me a copy of my signed contract immediately and quit making threats!

credit card company: Wait, i never made any threats. You will have to write to another address for a copy of the contract.

Joe: If you expect to get paid, you better find it and mail it to me. I'm not writing any more letters. I'll offer you a 20% settlement to close out the account and stop the harassment. When you are interested, please call me back. Bye!

Remember, they are desperately trying to get money out of you. You are the one in control. They can't get the money unless you give it to them. Normally, hold out for 20%, but you can accept a 30% counter offer if you want to make some deals quickly. I did this with HSBC because I knew Dell, GE Money and Capital One were going to try to play hardball. Just don't go over 30%. Keep in mind when these credit card companies have to sell the debt to a junk debt buyer, they will be getting 1-3 cents on the dollar. So you see, 30 cents on the dollar is a pretty good deal for everyone involved. If you want to save a little more money, you can offer 20%-30% on the principle balance only. Do this when the company is charging outrageous late fees and over the limit fees each month, causing your balance to go up substantially. In those cases, offer a settlement on the principle balance only, which does not include any of the ridiculous fees. Note: try to add in the words "threats" and "harassment" every so often. It can cause some of these bill collectors to squirm a little. Remember, customers sue bill collectors and file complaints, too.

Check out the link below to see a list of all of the banks that got the TARP money. $700 billion dollars going to over 600 companies. Remember, that's your money the government is giving away! And this does not include the $7.7 trillion in undisclosed loans these banks received. Even Congress was unaware of that dirty little secret!

http://www.nytimes.com/packages/html/national/200904_CREDITCRISIS/recipients.html

Back to your debt. When the credit card company does finally make a good settlement, you can set it up in 3 payments, 1 payment per month with the funds coming out of your bank account automatically. The first payment will need to be made within 10 days. A supervisor will confirm all of this over the phone. You will have to agree to this new contract. Note: only do this with the original creditor, the company that took the risk and gave you the credit. NEVER GIVE OUT YOUR BANK INFORMATION TO A COLLECTION AGENCY! They violate the laws all the time. They could clear out your bank account and then sell the debt to another buyer and claim you never paid. Collection agencies and junk debt buyers are for the most part the scum of the earth. Do not trust them. Never give them any of your private information, especially your financial information, where you work, or where you bank at. We will talk more about this in the collection agency section.

Let's look at some of the settlement confirmation letters from original creditors. These deals were all made for 20% - 30%. These original creditors were much easier to deal with than others, so hopefully you have cards from some of these companies.

Bank of America
www.bankofamerica.com

February 11, 2011

Account No.: ███████████

Dear ████████:

This letter confirms our agreement to settle the above-referenced account.

The balance at the time of settlement agreement was $1,887.82. We will accept $380.00 to settle this account.

Below are the payment terms for your account:

Due date	Payment amount	Due date	Payment amount
02/28/2011	$70.00		
03/31/2011	$310.00		

Upon receipt of all required payments, your account will be considered settled. You will not be obligated to pay the difference between the outstanding balance as of the time of settlement and the settlement amount. Your account has been closed to further charging privileges. Also, any future account activity that results in a credit balance may become the property of Bank of America. If a payment is returned for any reason, or if you fail to make required payments on time your settlement will be voided. Additionally, if any of these scenarios occur, the entire balance will be charged-off and we will continue to pursue the remaining debt.

01 of 02

Bank of America

www.bankofamerica.com

April 01, 2011

Account No.: ████████████

Dear ████████████

Thank you for your final payment toward the settlement of $320.00 for the above referenced account. This payment serves as the full settlement and your account will be reported to the consumer-reporting agencies (Experian, TransUnion, and Equifax) as a settled account, paid for less than the full balance. Any future credit balances on the account will be the property of Bank of America.

As a reminder, if the amount Bank of America has forgiven is equal to or greater than $600.00, we are required by federal law (IRS section 6050P) to report this amount to the IRS and issue a Form 1099-C. You will receive this form for the year in which the settlement completed. We recommend that you consult a certified public accountant or other tax professional if you have any questions regarding your personal taxes.

Although this account is now closed, please note that any new or third party charges posted to this account will be your responsibility. If this account is linked to any new charges or preauthorized third party fees or services such as, internet services or gym memberships, other charges may still post to the account. It is your responsibility to cancel any third party services that may or may not require authorization to charge the account. If any payments are returned for insufficient funds, the settlement will be voided. Once voided, unless previously charged-off, your account will be charged-off immediately and we will continue to pursue the debt.

████████████

01 of 02

FIA CARD SERVICES™
www.fiacardservices.com

▮▮▮▮▮▮▮▮▮▮▮ ▮▮▮▮▮▮▮▮

February 11, 2011

Account No.: ▮▮▮▮▮▮▮▮

Dear ▮▮▮▮▮▮▮

This letter confirms our agreement to settle the above-referenced account.

The balance at the time of settlement agreement was $8,988.49. We will accept $1,800.00 to settle this account.

Below are the payment terms for your account:

Due date	Payment amount	Due date	Payment amount
02/28/2011	$300.00		
03/31/2011	$1,500.00		

Upon receipt of all required payments, your account will be considered settled. You will not be obligated to pay the difference between the outstanding balance as of the time of settlement and the settlement amount. Your account has been closed to further charging privileges. Also, any future account activity that results in a credit balance may become the property of FIA Card Services. If a payment is returned for any reason, or if you fail to make required payments on time your settlement will be voided. Additionally, if any of these scenarios occur, the entire balance will be charged-off and we will continue to pursue the remaining debt.

▮▮▮▮▮▮▮

01 of 02

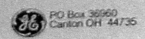

PO Box 36960
Canton OH 44735

GE Money Bank

March 8, 2011

Re: Account ████████████████

Confirmation # ███████████

This letter is a confirmation of a transaction you verbally authorized by telephone to make payment on the account listed above.

Details regarding the transaction appear below:

Payment Amount:	$111.00
Check Date:	03/18/11
Check Number:	3339
Drawn On:	███████████████ Bank

As discussed, the check drafted to make this payment will draw funds from your checking account. If you receive your cancelled checks, this check will be included in your statement. Please retain this letter for your records.

If this is a postdated check, this letter is to notify you that the check you sent will be deposited on the date indicated on the check. If you want to have this check deposited on a date other than what is on the check, you should contact our office during normal business hours no later than 3 days prior to the date of the check.

If for any reason, your bank will not be able to cover this check, it is your responsibility to notify us at the telephone number shown below.

Express Payment Dept.
GE Money Bank
P.O. Box 36960
Canton, Ohio 44735

Or call

(800) 541-9049

Thank You

This is an attempt to collect a debt and any information obtained will be used for that purpose.

A GE Money Bank Company

If you accept a settlement offer from the original creditor, be sure not to bounce any checks. If you do, and a payment has been declined, the deal is off, and you have to start the process all over again. The creditor will keep your money, of course, and apply it just like a regular payment on the account. Plus, the statute of limitations has now started over and you have wasted months, if not years of hard work getting to this point.

A WORD ABOUT CREDIT CARD RELIEF COMPANIES

If you have spent any time listening to the radio over the last few years, you have probably heard ads from companies claiming to offer credit card relief or debt settlements. They promise to stop the calls, and end the anguish that comes from dealing with your creditors. You have to be very careful when dealing with these companies, especially ones the Federal Trade Commission has gone after. Often, these companies will offer your creditors 50% settlements, and then tack on their own fees. In the end, your debts will be settled for around 65% of what you owe, which is incredibly high. You don't need a company to get a bad deal like that. You can do that all by yourself. So if you call up one of these companies, find out what the average settlement percentage is. Also find out what their fees are, if they offer any guarantees, do they offer refunds, and what happens if you get sued. Remember, a credit card company can refuse their offer and still try to sue you. And if that happens, you could end up paying the credit card company in full AND the debt relief company. Be sure to check for reviews online, and also with the Better Business Bureau before dealing with any of these companies.

Ripoffreport.com is a great website for reviewing questionable companies. Here is an example (from ripoffreport.com) of a debt relief company with some terrible reviews.

debt relief usa | Ripoff Report Directory | Complaints Reviews Scams Lawsuits Frauds Reported

Company Directory | debt relief usa

Approximately **40 Reports Found**
Showing 1 - 25

Wondering if a report is missing? We DO NOT remove reports from our database. However, as the leading consumer advocacy website, our technology is being continually upgraded to handle the volume of searches from consumers, the media, the authorities and millions of others from around the world. While we are always in the process of upgrading, our search results may not return all reports. This is only temporary and intermittent. If you are an attorney helping victims, the media, or law-enforcement, please contact us to have us run a complete database search to help your case or story.

Read how Rip-off Report protects consumers 1st amendment rights to speak out

Date	Title	City, State
12/29/2009 12:02 PM	DEBT RELIEF USASome got their money where's mine? Any updates? Addison, Texas Credit & Debt Services: DEBT RELIEF USA Texas	Author: Providence Rhode Island
8/1/2009 11:37 PM	Debt Relief USA , Inc. Gave $700 @ month to pay off creditors in a 2 year period. Approximatly $2000 uncounted for if not more? Addison Texas Miscellaneous Companies: Debt Relief USA , Inc. Texas	Author: Hemet California
7/19/2009 3:36 PM	Debt Relief USA is bankrupt, I WANT MY $$ BACK. Addison Texas Credit & Debt Services: Debt Relief USA Texas	Author: Las Vegas Nevada
6/29/2009 11:17 PM	Debt Relief USA Addison Texas Debt Relief USA screwed me in a bad way! Addison Texas Miscellaneous Companies: Debt Relief USA	Author: Columbia City Indiana

PAYING TAXES AFTER MAKING A SETTLEMENT

After you have settled a debt with your creditor, you are not out of the woods just yet. The government is going to want to take a cut of your settlement, too. If you have more than $600 of forgiven debt, you will have to file a 1099-C (cancellation of debt) form with the IRS. This forgiven debt is considered income, and will have to be declared on your federal income tax return. In other words, if you owed $10,000, and made a settlement for $2000, then you earned an extra $8000 in income this year. The creditor will mail you a tax form after the debt is considered paid in full. Below is a tax statement that shows $7188.49 that was forgiven by Bank of America.

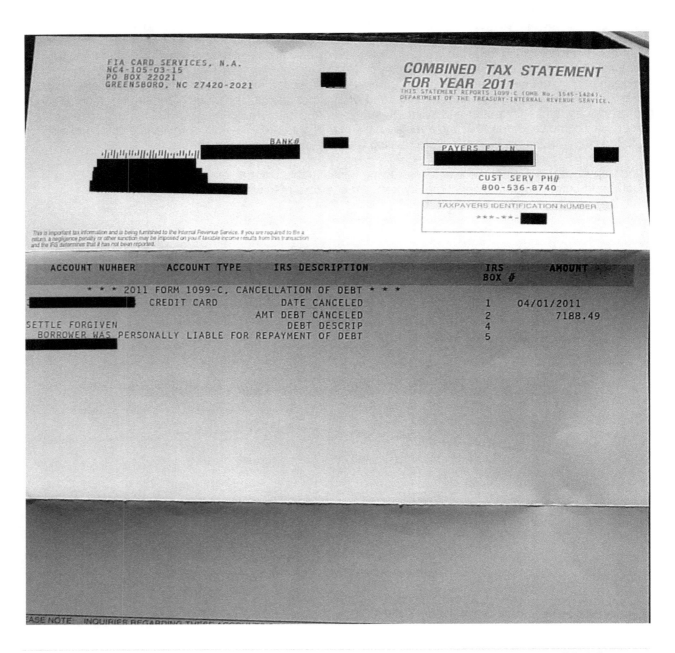

STEP 3 – DEALING WITH COLLECTION AGENCIES

Note: This next section is very important for you to read!!! Dealing with collection agencies is NOT like dealing with your original creditors. Original creditors will most likely obey state and federal laws. Collection agencies, on the other hand, will do anything to get t your money, and many will even break the law in the process. They have been known to harass relatives and neighbors, call your work, call early in the morning or late at night, and even tell your kids that they will take their toys if mommy doesn't pay her bills. There are plenty of horror stories online regarding the illegal actions of collection agencies, so it is very important that you do some research on any bill collector that is contacting you. You need to find out what their game plan is. Do they sue people, or do they just make threats over the phone and in collection letters? Have they been reported to the Federal Trade Commission, or Better Business Bureau? Before I describe how to deal with the collection agencies, you must first understand how these bottom feeders operate.

A collection agency will either **buy your bad debt**, or be **assigned your bad debt** from the original creditor. If the original creditor is sick of dealing with you, they might sell your debt for around 2-5 cents on the dollar to a junk debt buyer, or a collection agency. Here is the distinction. A **junk debt buyer** will buy a huge portfolio of devalued debts and try to collect the full amount on them. Specifically, they are buying the "media," or the documents needed to prove that they own the debt. They can buy a few accounts or a million dollars worth of accounts all at once. The accounts that are harder to collect on can be sold to other collection agencies, which can then be sold to even more collection agencies. This process can take years in some cases before the debt is resolved. The problem for the junk debt buyers is that they often can't get enough information from the original creditor to win their cases in court. That is why they must rely on default judgments when litigation comes into play. However, even if these debts are too old or uncollectable, it is still easy for the junk debt buyers to make money if they can con just a few of the debtors to pay them the full amount. Their main weapons are harassment, threats, lies, and fear. And they usually work on people that don't know the laws. Here's the proof. Debt buyers spend over $100 billion each year for bad debts. And with the recent economic recession, expect them to buy even more over the next few years. Debt buying = big money.

Here are a few notices I received from a collection company called Cavalry Portfolio Services, LLC. They purchased an alleged debt from HSBC Bank. You will find that most of these letters pretty much say the same thing, "this is an attempt to collect a debt" and "you have 30 days to dispute it in writing."

PO Box 1917
Hawthorne, NY 10532

███████████

███ MAY 06, 2011

ılıllıuıılıllılı ████████████████

RE: Original Institution: HSBC Bank Nevada, N.A. \
Orchard Bank
Original Account No.:
Cavalry Reference No.:
Balance Due: ████████

Dear ████████

This letter serves as notice that the above-referenced account has been purchased by Cavalry SPV I, LLC and referred to Cavalry Portfolio Services, LLC for collection.

It is important that you:

➤ Contact us to arrange repayment terms (however, see your validation rights below).
➤ Forward all future payments to the above address in order to ensure proper credit and avoid delays in payment posting.

Unless you notify this office within (30) days after the receipt of this letter that you dispute the validity of the debt or any portion thereof, this office will assume the debt is valid.

If you notify this office in writing within (30) days after receipt of this letter that you dispute all or a portion of the debt, this office will obtain verification of the debt or a copy of a judgment and mail you a copy of such judgment or verification.

If you request, in writing, within thirty (30) days of receiving this notice, Cavalry will provide you with the name and address of the original creditor.

If you have any questions or would like to discuss payment solutions you may call me directly at (877) 717-0188.

This communication is from a debt collector. This is an attempt to collect a debt and any information obtained will be used for that purpose.

Sincerely,

Linda Stiles Meyer

Cavalry Portfolio Services, LLC

"See Reverse Side for Important Information Concerning Your Rights"

PO Box 1017
Hawthorne, NY 10532

Phone: (877) 717-0188
www.cavalryportfolioservices.com

May 6, 2011

██████████

||,|||,|||,||,,||

RE: Original Institution: HSBC Bank Nevada, N.A. \
Orchard Bank
Original Account No.: ████████
Cavalry Account No.: ████████
Outstanding Balance: $710.10

Dear ████████

This letter serves as notice that the above-referenced account has been purchased by Cavalry Investments, LLC from HSBC Bank Nevada, N.A. and has been referred to Cavalry Portfolio Services, LLC ("Cavalry") for collection.

It is important that you:

➢ Contact us to arrange repayment terms (however, see your validation rights below).
➢ Forward all future payments to the above address in order to ensure proper credit and avoid delays in payment posting.

Unless you notify this office within 30 days after receiving this notice that you dispute the validity of this debt or any portion thereof, this office will assume this debt is valid.

If you notify this office in writing within 30 days from receiving this notice that you dispute the validity of this debt or any portion thereof, this office will obtain verification of the debt or obtain a copy of a judgment and mail you a copy of such judgment or verification.

If you request this office in writing within 30 days after receiving this notice this office will provide you with the name and address of the original creditor.

If you have any questions or would like to discuss payment solutions you may speak to a Customer Service Representative to resolve your account by calling us toll free at (877) 717-0188.

Sincerely,

Linda Stiles Meyer

> **THIS IS AN ATTEMPT TO COLLECT A DEBT. ANY INFORMATION OBTAINED WILL BE USED FOR THAT PURPOSE. THIS COMMUNICATION IS FROM A DEBT COLLECTOR. SEE REVERSE SIDE FOR IMPORTANT INFORMATION CONCERNING YOUR RIGHTS**

PAYMENT COUPON

Please detach and return this portion with your payment in the enclosed envelope. Be sure the address below shows through the return envelope window.

Make Checks and Money Orders Payable to
Cavalry Portfolio Services, LLC.

Cavalry Account No.:	████████
Outstanding Balance:	$710.10

Cavalry Portfolio Services, LLC
PO Box 27288
Tempe, AZ 85285-7288

Here is a notice from Enhanced Recovery Company, LLC. They were apparently assigned the debt by another debt buyer. ERC even put the Better Business Bureau logo on their form. According to bbb.org, they had 329 closed complaints in the last three years.

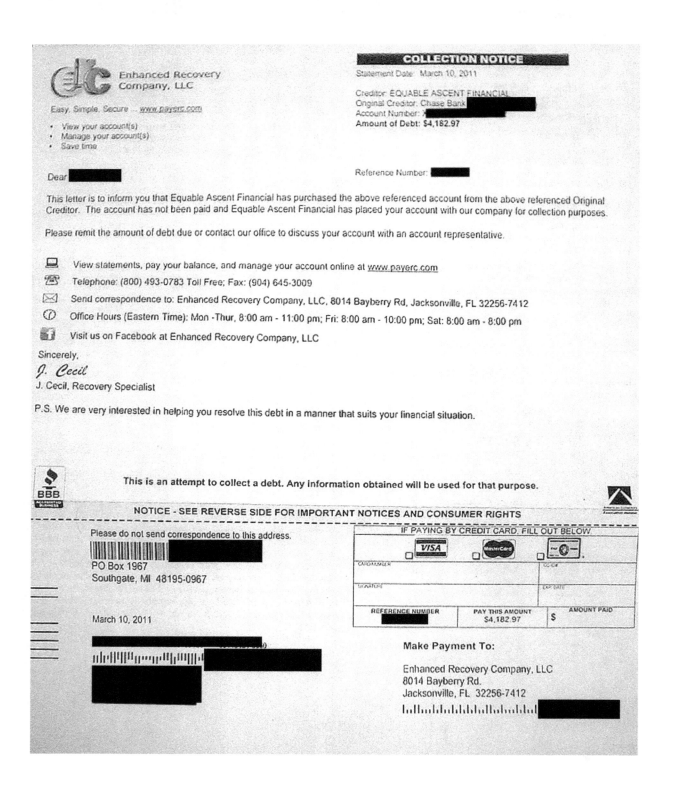

Here are the specifics from bbb.org, listed under the 32256 area code.

Customer Complaints Summary

329 complaints closed with BBB in last 3 years | 158 closed in last 12 months

Complaint Type	Total Closed Complaints
Advertising/Sales Issues	3
Billing/Collection Issues	250
Delivery Issues	4
Guarantee/Warranty Issues	0
Problems with Product/Service	72
Total Closed Complaints	329

Complaint Details | Definitions | BBB Complaint Process | File a Complaint

Complaint Breakdown by Resolution

Complaint Resolution Log (329)   BBB Closure Definitions

Complaint resolved with BBB assistance (307)

6/28/2011	Billing/Collection Issues
6/24/2011	Billing/Collection Issues
6/24/2011	Billing/Collection Issues
6/23/2011	Billing/Collection Issues
6/22/2011	Billing/Collection Issues
6/22/2011	Problems with Product/Service
6/22/2011	Billing/Collection Issues
6/21/2011	Billing/Collection Issues
6/19/2011	Billing/Collection Issues
6/18/2011	Billing/Collection Issues

1 2 3 4 5 6 7 8 9 10 ... 31

The debt buyer was Equable Ascent Financial. They assigned the debt to ERC.

COLLECTION NOTICE

Statement Date: March 10, 2011

Creditor: EQUABLE ASCENT FINANCIAL
Original Creditor: Chase Bank USA, N.A (WAMU)
Account Number: ▮▮▮▮▮▮▮▮▮▮▮
Amount of Debt: $4,182.97

Reference Number: 4▮▮▮▮▮▮

purchased the above referenced account from the above referenced Original
Financial has placed your account with our company for collection purposes.

scuss your account with an account representative.

Now let's talk about **assignees**. Before the debt is sold, the original creditor will usually try to get the money from an assignee. Most of the time the assignees are outside companies, but sometimes they can be an in house company owned by the original creditor. If a collection agency is assigned the debt from the original creditor, it just means that they were hired to send nasty letters and make phone calls. If they get the money, they make a percentage of what they collect. Or they can be paid a flat fee for the calls and letters that are sent out. Remember, assignees have no legal rights to your money or personal information! Yet, that won't stop some of them from trying to sue you and hope you don't show up in court or answer your summons. This happens all the time. They end up getting default judgments on thousands of cases that they never should have won. That is why it is so important to let these idiots know that you not only know about the law, but you are ready to fight them in court if needed.

On the next page you will see some examples of typical assignee collection agency letters. They all pretty much say the same thing. "You owe our client this much money, and you have 30 days to dispute the debt."

AlliedInterstate.
866-526-7795

BUFFALO	COLUMBUS	LOS ANGELES	PHOENIX
CAMBRIDGE	DELHI	MANILA	TORONTO
CLARK	HOUSTON	MINNEAPOLIS	WEST PALM BEACH

March 14, 2011

Re: Capital One Services Inc Account No. ████████
        Amount Owed $635.53

Dear █████████

We are a debt collection company and our client, Capital One Services Inc, has retained us to collect the debt noted above.

To make a payment, please telephone us at 866-526-7795 or mail your payment using the coupon on the reverse side of this letter.

The purpose of this letter is to collect this debt, and we will use any information we obtain for that purpose. If you believe that you do not owe all or any portion of the debt, you need to notify us within 30 days after receiving this letter. If you do not, we will assume the debt is valid. If you notify us in writing within 30 days after receiving this letter that you dispute the validity of any portion of this debt, we will obtain verification of the debt, or a copy of a judgment against you, and mail it to you. If you provide a written request within 30 days after receiving this letter, we will provide you with the name and address of the original creditor, if different from the current creditor.

We urge you to make this payment promptly. If you fail to do so, we will have no choice but to continue taking further actions to ensure our client is paid.

Sincerely,

Allied Interstate LLC

— RECEIVED 3/21
— MAILED OUT 3/22
TO ~~████~~ ADDRESS +
CAPITAL ONE ADDRESS
+ ~~████████~~ IL.

SEE REVERSE SIDE FOR OTHER IMPORTANT INFORMATION

PO Box 12100
DEPT 64
Trenton, NJ 08650

‖‖‖‖‖‖‖‖‖‖‖‖‖‖‖‖‖‖ ████████████

4740 Baxter Road
Virginia Beach VA 23462

NCO FINANCIAL SYSTEMS INC

1-866-401-2139
OFFICE HOURS (ALL TIMES EASTERN)
8AM-9PM MON FRIDAY
8AM-6PM SATURDAY
10AM-9PM SUNDAY
Feb 13, 2011

‖‖‖‖‖‖‖‖‖‖‖‖‖‖‖‖‖‖‖ ████████ ████████

Creditor: CAPITAL ONE BANK (USA), N.A.
Account #: ██████████
Total Balance: $ 606.52

The above named creditor has placed this account with our office for collection. You can use your tax refund or company bonus to pay this account. Send payment in full to the address listed below. You can also contact us concerning a settlement for less than the full balance of the account. You may contact us at 1-866-401-2139 for details.

You may also make payment by visiting http://www.capitalone.com/solutions.

Unless you notify this office within 30 days after receiving this notice that you dispute the validity of the debt or any portion thereof, this office will assume this debt is valid. If you notify this office in writing within 30 days of receiving this notice, this office will obtain verification of the debt or obtain a copy of a judgment and mail you a copy of such judgment or verification. If you request this office in writing within 30 days after receiving this notice, this office will provide you with the name and address of the original creditor, if different from the current creditor.

Sincerely,

NCO Financial Systems, Inc.

Calls to or from this company may be monitored or recorded for quality assurance.

This is an attempt to collect a debt. Any information obtained will be used for that purpose. This is a communication from a debt collector.

PLEASE RETURN THIS PORTION WITH YOUR PAYMENT (MAKE SURE ADDRESS SHOWS THROUGH WINDOW)

0000000 0 ████████████████)0000000

Please print address changes below using blue or black ink

Street		Apt. #
City	State	ZIP
Home Phone	Alternate Phone	

Balance $ 606.52

Total Enclosed $ [   ]

‖‖‖‖‖‖‖‖‖‖‖‖‖‖‖‖‖‖ ████████
CAPITAL ONE BANK (USA), N.A.
PO Box 71083
Charlotte NC 28272-1083

PO Box 101926, Dept. 3417
Birmingham, AL 35210

▌▊▋▊▐ ███

April 18, 2011

ı.ı.ıll.ıll..ı..l.ıl.ıl.ıll.ı.ılll..
███ ED AADC 350

CREDIT&COLLECTIONCORP
Global Credit & Collection Corp.
300 International Drive
PMB #10015
Williamsville, NY 14221
1-866-350-7727

Client:	Equable Ascent Financial, LLC
Original Creditor:	Washington Mutual Card
Account Number:	
Global ID:	
Amount Due:	$1805.68

Dear ███,

Your account has been placed with Global Credit & Collection Corp., a collection agency.

I must advise you that your account has met the criteria for possible legal action by Equable Ascent Financial, LLC. To avoid potentially being sued and possibly save money resulting from attorney fees, court costs or collection fees, contact our office at the toll free number provided below.

As soon as we receive your payment in full on the above-noted account all collection activity will be stopped. All payments mailed to this office should be payable to Global Credit & Collection Corp.

Should you have any questions concerning your payment or your account, please telephone our office. Please make sure that your payment clearly identifies your name and that of Equable Ascent Financial, LLC so that payment can be properly applied to your account.

Mr. Duarte
1-866-350-7727

SEE REVERSE SIDE FOR IMPORTANT INFORMATION.
Detach and Return Bottom Portion with Payment

Pay by Credit Card

Fill in all of the information below

☐ VISA	☐	☐ DISCVER
Card #		Security Code	Expiration Date
Billing Address		
Signature	Amount Authorized $	

Pay by Auto Pay Payment

Fill in all of the information below, and we will arrange this payment free of charge

Name of Bank	☐ Checking	☐ Savings
Routing Number	Account Number	Payment Date
Name of Account Holder		
Signature	Amount Authorized $	

Client:	Equable Ascent Financial, LLC
Original Creditor:	Washington Mutual Card
Account Number:	
Global ID:	
Amount Due:	$1805.68

ıı·ıl·ıı·l·lıılı··ıl·ılll··ll··lı·lll·lllıllı·llll
Global Credit & Collection Corp.
300 International Drive
SUITE 100, PMB #10015
Williamsville, NY 14221

HC

1-866-350-7727

Redline Recovery

Date: February 26, 2011

[REDACTED]

STATEMENT
Account Summary
Current Creditor: HSBC BANK
Reference:
Account ID [REDACTED]
Balance: $696.09

Dear [REDACTED]

Your account has been placed with our office for collection.

Because your account is in default, the entire amount of $696.09 is due. Failure to make payment will result in our agency's continued collection efforts.

As of the date of this letter, you owe $696.09. Because of interest, late charges, and other charges that may vary from day to day, the amount due on the day you pay may be greater. Hence if you pay the amount shown above, an adjustment may be necessary after we receive your payment. If an adjustment is made, we may attempt to contact you again about the adjustment. For further information, please write us or call 1-866-388-1224

Unless you notify this office within 30 days after receiving this notice that you dispute the validity of this debt or any portion thereof, this office will assume this debt is valid. If you notify this office in writing within 30 days from receiving this notice that you dispute the validity of this debt or any portion thereof, this office will obtain verification of the debt or obtain a copy of a judgment and mail you a copy of such judgment or verification. If you request of this office in writing within 30 days after receiving this notice this office will provide you with the name and address of the original creditor, if different from the current creditor.

This is an attempt to collect a debt and any information obtained will be used for that purpose. This is a communication from a debt collector.

PLEASE RESPOND

TELEPHONE: 1-866-388-1224

Pay online by check, credit card, or debit card at www.redlinepayment.com.

Please include your Account ID, H4358508, with all payments and correspondence sent to:
REDLINE RECOVERY SERVICES, LLC., 11675 RAINWATER DR STE 350, ALPHARETTA GA 30009-8693

Office Hours: Mon. - Thur. 7:30 AM - 9:00 PM CST; Fri. - Sat. 7:30AM - 4:30 PM CST; Sun. 1:00 PM - 8:00 PM CST

PLEASE DETACH HERE AND RETURN WITH YOUR PAYMENT TO THE ADDRESS PRINTED BELOW

Date: February 26, 2011

[REDACTED]

If paying by Credit Card, please complete this section			
CARD NUMBER		AMOUNT	CVV # (3 or 4 Digit) code on Back of Card
VISA	SIGNATURE	EXP DATE	
CARDHOLDER NAME (Please Print)			Check Here if Cardholder Address is The Same - if Not, Provide Cardholder Address On Back of Statement

STATEMENT
Account Summary
Current Creditor: HSBC BANK
Reference: [REDACTED]
Account ID [REDACTED]
Balance: $696.09

Please send your payment or correspondence to:
REDLINE RECOVERY SERVICES, LLC.
11675 RAINWATER DR STE 350
ALPHARETTA GA 30009-8693

PAY THIS AMOUNT $696.09

Van Ru Credit Corporation
1350 E Touhy Ave Suite 100E
Des Plaines IL 60018-3307
866-379-8649

PO Box 46549
Lincolnwood IL 60646-0549
RETURN SERVICE REQUESTED

March 28, 2011

Van Ru
PO Box 46249
Lincolnwood IL 60646

File #: ████████
Balance: $792.09

Detach Upper Portion And Return With Payment

Creditor: DSNB/Macy's
Account #:   ████████
Balance: $792.09

The above account has been placed with us for collection. This is an important matter and deserves your immediate attention.

Your payment, made payable to Department Store National Bank, may be mailed in the enclosed envelope. If you have any questions, or wish to discuss your account with one of our representatives, you may call us toll-free at 866-379-8649.

Unless you notify this office within 30 days after receiving this notice that you dispute the validity of this debt or any portion thereof, this office will assume this debt is valid. If you notify this office in writing within 30 days from receiving this notice that you dispute the validity of this debt or any portion thereof, this office will obtain verification of the debt or obtain a copy of a judgment and mail you a copy of such judgment or verification. If you request this office in writing within 30 days after receiving this notice, this office will provide you with the name and address of the original creditor, if different from the current creditor.

This communication is from a debt collector. This is an attempt to collect a debt. Any information obtained will be used for that purpose.

Yours truly,

Van Ru Credit Corporation

Van Ru Credit Corporation ◆ 1350 E Touhy Ave Suite 100E ◆ Des Plaines IL 60018-3307 ◆ 866-379-8649
Mon-Thu 7am to 9pm Fri 8am to 5pm Sat 8am to 12pm CT

Note: there are also collection law firms that are in the business of collecting debts. Often, these companies have one lawyer on board to sign their letters. It appears intimidating to get a letter from a collection lawyer, but in reality, these are still just your average collection agency. It doesn't matter who wrote the letter. When you do research on the collection agency that contacts you, you will be able to determine if it is a local law firm that is about to sue you, or just another assignee or junk debt buyer. Take a look at this next example. You would assume by looking at it, that this notice is from licensed attorneys.

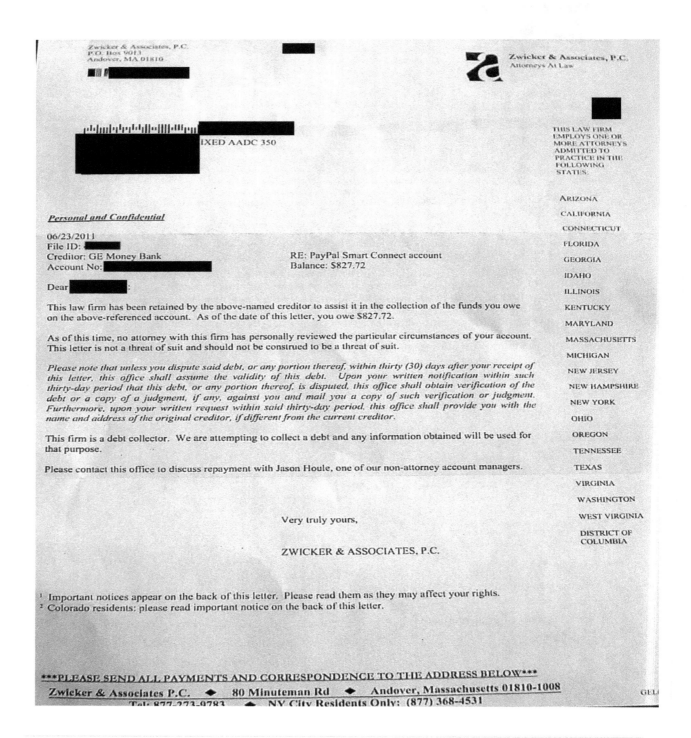

Zwicker & Associates, P.C.
P.O. Box 9013
Andover, MA 01810

Zwicker & Associates, P.C.
Attorneys At Law

THIS LAW FIRM EMPLOYS ONE OR MORE ATTORNEYS ADMITTED TO PRACTICE IN THE FOLLOWING STATES:

ARIZONA
CALIFORNIA
CONNECTICUT
FLORIDA
GEORGIA
IDAHO
ILLINOIS
KENTUCKY
MARYLAND
MASSACHUSETTS
MICHIGAN
NEW JERSEY
NEW HAMPSHIRE
NEW YORK
OHIO
OREGON
TENNESSEE
TEXAS
VIRGINIA
WASHINGTON
WEST VIRGINIA
DISTRICT OF COLUMBIA

IXED AADC 350

Personal and Confidential

06/23/2011
File ID:
Creditor: GE Money Bank
Account No:

RE: PayPal Smart Connect account
Balance: $827.72

Dear   :

This law firm has been retained by the above-named creditor to assist it in the collection of the funds you owe on the above-referenced account. As of the date of this letter, you owe $827.72.

As of this time, no attorney with this firm has personally reviewed the particular circumstances of your account. This letter is not a threat of suit and should not be construed to be a threat of suit.

Please note that unless you dispute said debt, or any portion thereof, within thirty (30) days after your receipt of this letter, this office shall assume the validity of this debt. Upon your written notification within such thirty-day period that this debt, or any portion thereof, is disputed, this office shall obtain verification of the debt or a copy of a judgment, if any, against you and mail you a copy of such verification or judgment. Furthermore, upon your written request within said thirty-day period, this office shall provide you with the name and address of the original creditor, if different from the current creditor.

This firm is a debt collector. We are attempting to collect a debt and any information obtained will be used for that purpose.

Please contact this office to discuss repayment with Jason Houle, one of our non-attorney account managers.

Very truly yours,

ZWICKER & ASSOCIATES, P.C.

[1] Important notices appear on the back of this letter. Please read them as they may affect your rights.
[2] Colorado residents: please read important notice on the back of this letter.

PLEASE SEND ALL PAYMENTS AND CORRESPONDENCE TO THE ADDRESS BELOW
Zwicker & Associates P.C. ◆ 80 Minuteman Rd ◆ Andover, Massachusetts 01810-1008
Tel: 877-273-9783 ◆ NY City Residents Only: (877) 368-4531

If you do a simple Google search, you will find some interesting posts regarding this company. In fact, one post from RipoffReport.com claimed that the owner of the company was disbarred in 2005. Just remember; always do research on the collection agency that is contacting you!

The post below was found at: http://www.ripoffreport.com/collection-agency-s/zwicker-associates/zwicker-associates-unwilling-f4c4w.htm

#7 Consumer Suggestion

Zwicker and Associates: Just another Collection Agency

AUTHOR: Bobbkat - Little Elm (U.S.A.)

SUBMITTED: Friday, March 06, 2009

Zwicker and Associates is nothing more than a nationwide Collection Agency, who's principle offices are located in the State of Massachusetts. If you don't live in their immediate area, it would be foolish to think they would file a Law Suit against anyone unless the debt in question is more than $3000.00 only because of the sheer cost involved. Also if you live in a 'Consumer Friendly State' such as Texas, New Jersey, Florida and North Carolina to mention a few, with no salary attachment laws, a law suit isn't going to happen no matter how much you owe.

PRESIDENT
Paul W. Zwicker admitted to bar, 1979, Massachusetts. Education: American International College (B.A., 1975); New York Law School (J.D., 1979). Practice Areas: Civil Litigation.

There's more about him elsewhere, such as news for the California Bar Association:

KENNETH D. ZWICKER 46, of Chatsworth CA, a relative and former associate of Zwicker and Associates was summarily disbarred Aug. 21, 2005, and was ordered to comply with rule 955 of the FDCPA.. Zwicker was also convicted of one count of mail fraud in 2003 and placed on interim suspension in 2004. Because the offense was a felony that involved moral turpitude, he was summarily disbarred

Bottom line: these clowns are not going to do anything but call you. Ignore them in whatever way you fell appropriate and eventually, they will move on to greener pastures.

Here is another interesting notice describing a class action lawsuit against Zwicker & Associates in 2007. This PDF file can be found here: http://www.quatlaw.com/classfiles/zwicker/Class_Notice.pdf

<u>NOTICE OF CLASS ACTION AND PROPOSED SETTLEMENT</u>
<u>("MEFA SETTLEMENT NOTICE")</u>

TO: All natural persons who reside in the United States of America: (a) who were sent a letter or letters from Zwicker & Associates, P.C. between July 17, 2000 through _____, 2007, in connection with an alleged debt owed to the Massachusetts Educational Financing Authority ("MEFA") and who, prior to litigation being commenced on said alleged debt, paid 100% of principal, accrued interest, and attorney's fees and/or collection costs allegedly owed as of the date final payment was made without receiving any itemization of that amount that included principal, interest, and costs (including attorney's fees, if applicable) before such payment.

PLEASE READ THIS NOTICE CAREFULLY.

THIS IS <u>NOT</u> AN ATTEMPT TO COLLECT MONEY FROM YOU.
THIS IS <u>NOT</u> A NOTICE OF A LAWSUIT <u>AGAINST</u> YOU.
<u>*YOU MAY BENEFIT FROM READING THIS NOTICE.*</u>

<u>WHY YOU ARE BEING SENT THIS NOTICE</u>

There is now pending in the United States District Court for the District of Massachusetts a class action lawsuit entitled <u>Feuerstein v. Zwicker & Associates, P.C., et al.</u>, Case No. 04-11593-WGY (the "Litigation"). This Notice explains the nature of the Litigation, general terms of a proposed settlement, and informs you of your legal rights and obligations.

Judge William G. Young of the United States District Court for the Eastern Division of Massachusetts has granted preliminary approval of a settlement agreement in the above-entitled action, subject to a hearing on the fairness of the settlement which will take place on _____, 2007 at ____ in Room 18 of the John Joseph Moakley United States Courthouse, 1 Courthouse Way, Suite 2300, Boston, MA 02210.

You are being sent this notice because you appear to be a member of the class defined above. This notice explains the nature of the lawsuit, the terms of the settlement, describes how you may benefit from the settlement and informs you of your legal rights, options, and obligations.

<u>WHAT THIS LAWSUIT IS ABOUT</u>

This lawsuit contends that Zwicker & Associates, P.C. ("Defendant") violated the Fair Debt Collection Practices Act ("FDCPA"). Plaintiff alleged that Defendant sent Plaintiff and class members debt collection letters that failed to properly itemize the amount of the debt which was or is allegedly owed to MEFA, including collection costs and/or attorney's fees that were added on to the original debt. As a result, Plaintiff alleges that class members paid collection costs and/or attorney's fees of which they were not aware.

Here is another webpage describing a lawsuit filed in 2011. Here is the source:
http://dockets.justia.com/docket/california/candce/4:2011cv03446/242969/

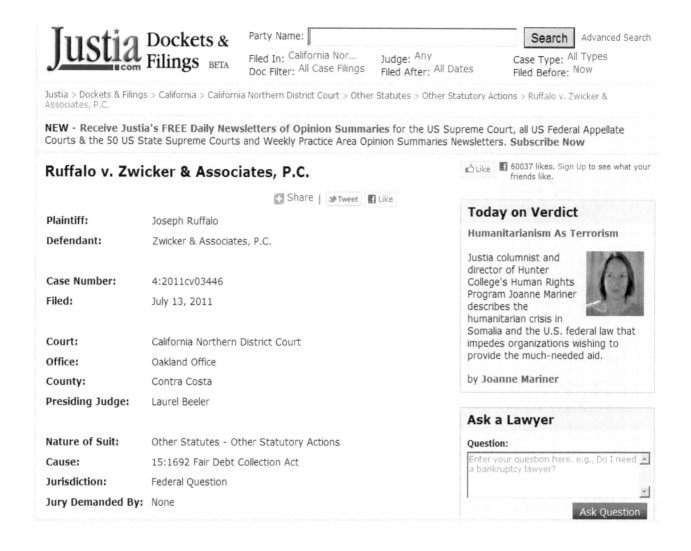

If you do a search on the Justia.com website you will find over 200 cases regarding Zwicker & Associates. And it looks like the cause of action is often the Fair Debt Collection Practices Act (FDCPA). If this company does in fact have attorneys on staff, then they just might be busy dealing with all of the lawsuits that are filed against them. Check out the image on the next page. Here is the source:
http://dockets.justia.com/search?query=zwicker+associates&page=5

You can use this site to search for cases filed against any collection agency. Find out who is suing them and why. So be sure to use RipoffReport.com and Justia.com when doing your research.

Cases filed matching "zwicker associates"

 RSS FEED View as Table

GOODMAN v. BANK OF AMERICA et al

Filed: July 19, 2011 as 1:2011cv00956

Plaintiff: CARL GOODMAN

Defendants: BANK OF AMERICA, WRIGHT & LERCH and ZWICKER & ASSOCIATES, PC.

Presiding Judge: William T. Lawrence

Referring Judge: Debra McVicker Lynch

Cause Of Action: Fair Debt Collection Act

Court: Seventh Circuit > Indiana > Southern District Court

Type: Other Statutes > Commerce ICC Rates, Etc.

Catti v. Zwicker & Associates, P.C. et al

Filed: July 15, 2011 as 2:2011cv03453

Plaintiff: Gary Catti

Defendants: Does 1-10 and Zwicker & Associates, P.C.

Presiding Judge: Joanna Seybert

Referring Judge: A. Kathleen Tomlinson

Cause Of Action: Fair Debt Collection Act

Court: Second Circuit > New York > Eastern District Court

Type: Other Statutes > Consumer Credit

Ruffalo v. Zwicker & Associates, P.C.

Filed: July 13, 2011 as 4:2011cv03446

Plaintiff: Joseph Ruffalo

Another weapon that the collection agencies use is skip tracing. This involves the use of investigative computer programs that search through your available personal records to gain information on your whereabouts. Even if the collection company already knows your name, address, and phone number, the skip tracer will provide them with additional information like any businesses you own, union memberships, previous addresses, relatives, neighbors, your kid's school, utility bills, phone bills, court records, credit reports, tax information, marriage licenses, voter registration, and more. Anything you have posted online with your name, email, or phone number can also be found, like your Myspace, Facebook, Linkedin, or Craigslist webpage.

The link below is an example of a basic skip tracer program. The collection agencies will have more advanced ones. I typed in my name in the public records search and the tracer knew my age, where I lived, and who I was related to. Type in your name and give it a try. Also, do a Google search for your name, phone number, and email address. You can bet that the collection agencies will be looking to see what comes up. They need to determine if you have money and how they can effectively harass you.

http://proagency.tripod.com/ask1.html

Note: Once you have stopped paying your credit cards, be wary of new friend requests on Facebook or any social networking site from individuals you don't know. The requests could be from a collection agency trying to get in touch with you or your friends. This type of humiliation usually forces a person to contact the collection agency and pay off the debt. So beware!

Here is another free tracer report. Enter your name and see what comes up.

http://www.spokeo.com

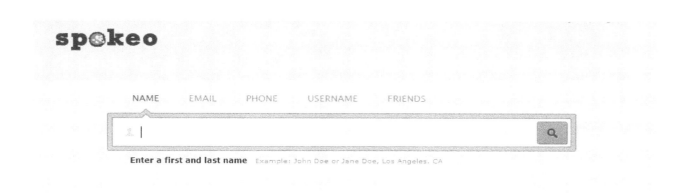

Here is a picture of the street outside of an apartment that I used to live at. A simple search of my name on Spokeo found this image, which was produced by Google. The main point here is that if you don't communicate with the collection agencies, either by phone or letter, the advanced skip tracers can find you, your family, and your friends.

Property Description

Find out all available property information for ****** E Kirkwood Ave.

Check out some of the websites that this basic skip tracer searches through. Imagine what the advanced ones can do. If you are on these sites, check their privacy policies. You don't want your posts or profile to be public if you are trying to avoid the collection agencies.

Major Social Networks	Blogging Sites	Photo Sharing
Bebo	LiveJournal	PhotoBucket
Hi5	AOL Lifestream	Picasa
Multiply	Blogger	Slide
MySpace	Disqus	Flickr
MyYearbook	Google Buzz	Gravatar
Tagged	Posterous	PictureTrail
Buzznet	Twitter	deviantART
Facebook	WordPress	Fotolog
IMVU	Xanga	ImageShack
Netlog	Tumblr	WebShots
BlackPlanet	Wretch	Behance
		SmugMug

Music Sites	Video Sites	Online Shopping
Jango	Flixster	Amazon
Pandora	Vimeo	Target
iLike	dailymotion	eBay
Lyrics	Hulu	Etsy
Last.fm	Justin TV	Zazzle
SoundCloud	Metacafe	Epinions

HOW TO FIGHT THE COLLECTION COMPANIES

Now it's time to make these companies go away. Most of the time it can be done in two simple steps. Both involve letters that you write. Once you have received a debt collection letter from a collection agency, you will need to send out a request for validation. You only have thirty days to dispute the debt, so you must act quickly. The validation request is a demand for proof that you owe a company a certain amount of money. Just because someone asks you for money, doesn't mean you owe them money. They have to prove it. This proof of debt is your right under the law, which applies to all collection agencies. If you look up the **Fair Debt Collection Practices Act (FDCPA)** it states that a debt collector must provide verification of the debt, and they cannot collect on the debt until validation is provided. What exactly is debt validation? The FDCPA doesn't really say. According to one court case, *Chaudhry v. Gallerizzo,* debt validation is nothing more than the name of the creditor and the amount owed. Remember, not all judges can be trusted. Most states, however, have contract laws and trial laws which are much stricter. Certain states require that the original contract from the original creditor must be present before you can be sued for breach of contract. After all, if there is a contract dispute, maybe on the interest or late fees charged, then the judge will need to see the very contract you signed contract to see what it says. The good news is that these contracts don't exist in 80%-90% of the cases. Often, older contracts are thrown out or shredded. And who knows what they do with the recordings of applicants signing up over the phone

If the collection company cannot provide you with a copy of the original signed contract from the original creditor (often because it doesn't exist anymore), then they will have to come up with an **Affidavit of Debt**. This is a form from the collection agency or original creditor that states that a certain employee is "intimately familiar with the methods of record keeping at the original creditor," and this employee claims that the debt is 100% accurate.

Here is an example from http://www.creditinfocenter.com

Plaintiff's Affidavit of Indebtedness and Ownership of Account

I am an Authorized representative for Acme Collection Agency (hereafter the "Plaintiff") and hereby certify as follows:

1. I have personal knowledge regarding plaintiff's creation and maintenance of its normal business records including computer records of its accounts receivables. This information was regularly and contemporaneously maintained during the course of the plaintiffs business. I am authorized to execute this affidavit on behalf of plaintiff and the information below is true and correct to the best of my knowledge, information and belief based on business records maintained with respect to the account.
2. The records provided to plaintiff have been represented to include information provided by the original creditor. Such information includes the debtors name, social security number, account balance, and identity of the original creditor and account number.
3. Based on the business records maintained on account XXXXXXXXXX (hereafter "account") which are a compilation of the information provided upon acquisition and information obtained since acquisition, the account is the result of the extension of credit to "name" by Original Creditor, on or about 6/16/03 (the "date of the origination"). Said business records further indicate that the account was then owned by Acme Huge Bank. Acme Huge Bank later sold and/or assigned portfolio 8044 to plaintiff's assignor which included the defendant's account on 7/3/2007 (the "Date of Assignment"). Thereafter, all ownership rights were assigned to, transferred to, and became vested in Plaintiff, including the right to collect the purchased balance owing $1487.64 plus any additional accrued interest.
4. To the best of my knowledge and belief, the defendant is not a minor or mentally incompetent.
5. Based on business records maintained in regard to the account, the above stated amounts is justly and duly owned by the defendant to the plaintiff and that all just and lawful offsets, payments, and credits to the account have been allowed. Demand for payment was made more than 30 days ago.

Signed,
Clueless Employee
Acme Collection Agency

The problem with these affidavits is that they are often falsified. The account expert does not exist. And in reality, the signatures come from employees hired to robo-sign thousands of phony affidavits. Chase Bank is just one example of a company that is being accused of robo-signing according to this AOL Daily Finance article: http://www.dailyfinance.com/2010/12/17/chase-sec-whistleblower-complaint-credit-card/

*1. Chase Bank sold to third party debt buyers hundreds of millions of dollars worth of credit card accounts. . .when in fact Chase Bank executives **knew** that many of those accounts had incorrect and overstated balances.*

*3. Chase Bank executives routinely **destroyed** information and communications from consumers rather than incorporate that information into the consumer's credit card file, including bankruptcy notices, powers of attorney, notice of cancellation of auto-pay, proof of payments and letters from debt settlement companies.*

*4. Chase Bank executives **mass-executed** thousands of affidavits in support of Chase Banks collection efforts and those Chase Bank executives did not have personal knowledge of the facts set forth in the affidavits.*

*5. When senior Chase Bank executives were made aware of these systemic problems, senior Chase Bank executives -- rather than remedy the problems -- immediately **fired** the whistleblower and attempted to cover up these problems.*

If you get sued, the best way to deal with a fake Affidavit of Debt is with a Motion to Strike filed in court. The affidavit is hearsay, because it is often signed by an employee of the collection agency and not the original creditor who actually monitored the debt. In other words, the expert who signed the affidavit (the affiant) doesn't know what they are talking about. If a motion to strike doesn't work, you can file a Sworn Denial. This forces the collection company to bring the account expert to court to testify in person. Chances are, the affiant is not an expert, and he or she never saw your contract. So the court case usually goes away. This will be discussed in more detail later on. The important thing to remember is that we will be showing the collection agencies (in the validation letter) that we want a fight. And this will prevent lawsuits. Think about it like this, if you are a walking down a dark alley with an M-16A2 rifle in your hands, it's pretty unlikely that someone is going to mess with you unless they have something bigger. But the collection agencies usually don't have anything bigger. That's why they have to resort to harassment and name calling. It's effective and it's all they got.

If the company that owns your debt actually has a copy of the original signed contract and can legally do business in your state, then you can begin to negotiate a settlement deal with them for 20% - 30%. If you come to an agreement, get it in writing first, and record all telephone conversations with them. Payments are to be made with money orders from anywhere EXCEPT your bank. Remember, NEVER trust collection agencies or junk debt buyers. They can take your money, and then turn around and sell your debt to another sleazy collector. Or they can take your settlement payments, and then sue you for the remainder of the debt. Remember, you should only make deals with whoever legally owns your debt. Hopefully, that is the original creditor. If not, you need to be ready to go to court with proof that you made a legal deal and paid off the debt. Some junk debt buyers will actually sue you and then call you up and make a deal for 10% - 20%. They will tell you not to bother going to court since a deal was made. Case dismissed. The only problem is that they never cancelled the court date, and they just got a default judgement against you for 100% of the amount owed because you never showed up to court. If you had been there, they probably would have lost the case. Do not trust anyone in the debt collection industry, especially if they can't prove anything. The ones with the least evidence are the most dangerous.

Take a look at this letter from GE Money. They don't have the original contract. Where did it go?

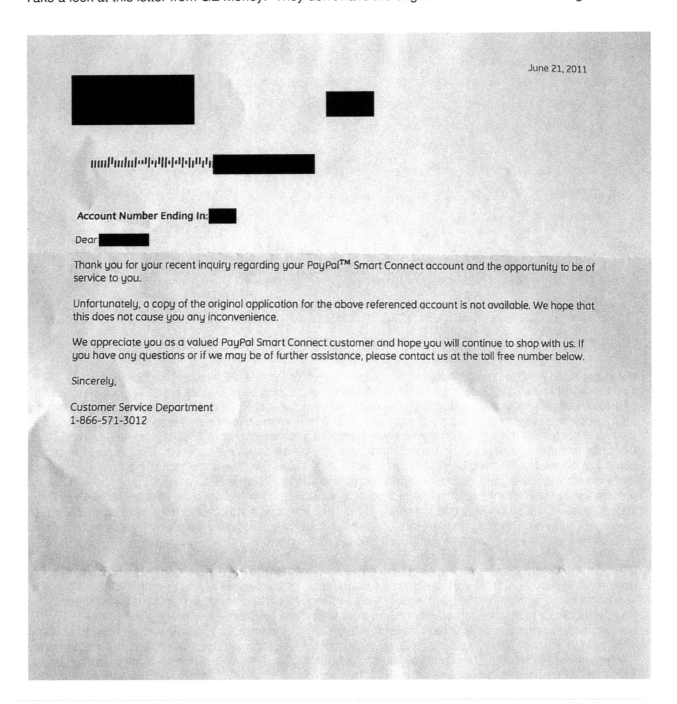

June 21, 2011

██████████████

███████

ıınıl¹ınlnl⋅⋅¹ı₁ıllı⋅l⋅l₁lⁱrl₁ ██████████

Account Number Ending In: ████

Dear ████████

Thank you for your recent inquiry regarding your PayPal™ Smart Connect account and the opportunity to be of service to you.

Unfortunately, a copy of the original application for the above referenced account is not available. We hope that this does not cause you any inconvenience.

We appreciate you as a valued PayPal Smart Connect customer and hope you will continue to shop with us. If you have any questions or if we may be of further assistance, please contact us at the toll free number below.

Sincerely,

Customer Service Department
1-866-571-3012

Here is another letter from GE Money. They still don't know how the alleged account was opened. They want a debtor to abide by the terms, but I have no "proof" of what they are. They are claiming that "signing" the application validated the contract, which means they will probably use "breach of contract" as a claim if this dispute ends up in litigation. Other credit card companies will state that "use" of the card validates the contract and then claim "account stated" (implied contract resulting from failure to dispute billing statements) in litigation.

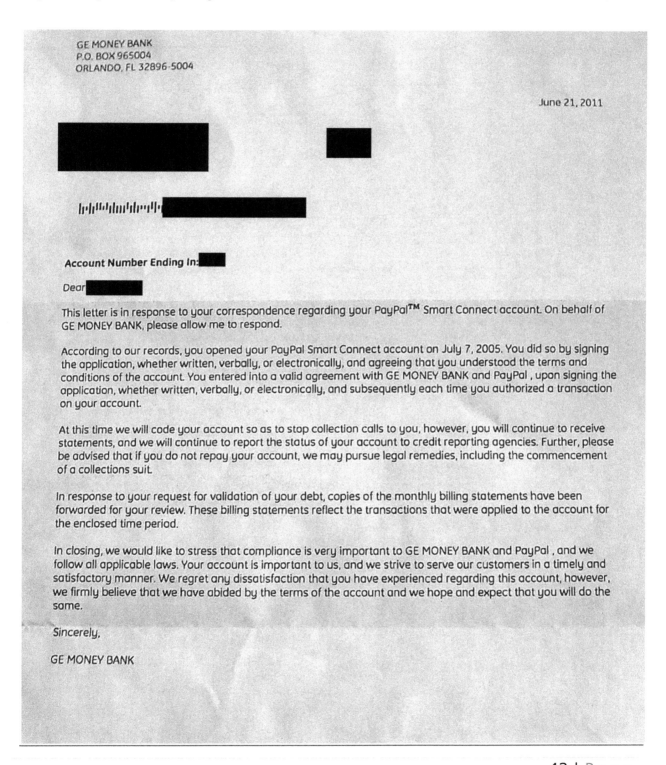

GE MONEY BANK
P.O. BOX 965004
ORLANDO, FL 32896-5004

June 21, 2011

Account Number Ending In:

Dear

This letter is in response to your correspondence regarding your PayPal™ Smart Connect account. On behalf of GE MONEY BANK, please allow me to respond.

According to our records, you opened your PayPal Smart Connect account on July 7, 2005. You did so by signing the application, whether written, verbally, or electronically, and agreeing that you understood the terms and conditions of the account. You entered into a valid agreement with GE MONEY BANK and PayPal , upon signing the application, whether written, verbally, or electronically, and subsequently each time you authorized a transaction on your account.

At this time we will code your account so as to stop collection calls to you, however, you will continue to receive statements, and we will continue to report the status of your account to credit reporting agencies. Further, please be advised that if you do not repay your account, we may pursue legal remedies, including the commencement of a collections suit.

In response to your request for validation of your debt, copies of the monthly billing statements have been forwarded for your review. These billing statements reflect the transactions that were applied to the account for the enclosed time period.

In closing, we would like to stress that compliance is very important to GE MONEY BANK and PayPal , and we follow all applicable laws. Your account is important to us, and we strive to serve our customers in a timely and satisfactory manner. We regret any dissatisfaction that you have experienced regarding this account, however, we firmly believe that we have abided by the terms of the account and we hope and expect that you will do the same.

Sincerely,

GE MONEY BANK

Note: if you receive a collection letter from a law firm in your town, be very careful. Often, agencies will hire local firms to sue you. When this happens, send out the validation letter, then file complaints against them to the FTC, State Attorney General, and BBB. This will be explained more in detail later on. Below is an example of a local attorney trying to collect a debt. The idea that your debt will change from day to day is probably illegal, unless specified somewhere on your original signed contract with the original creditor.

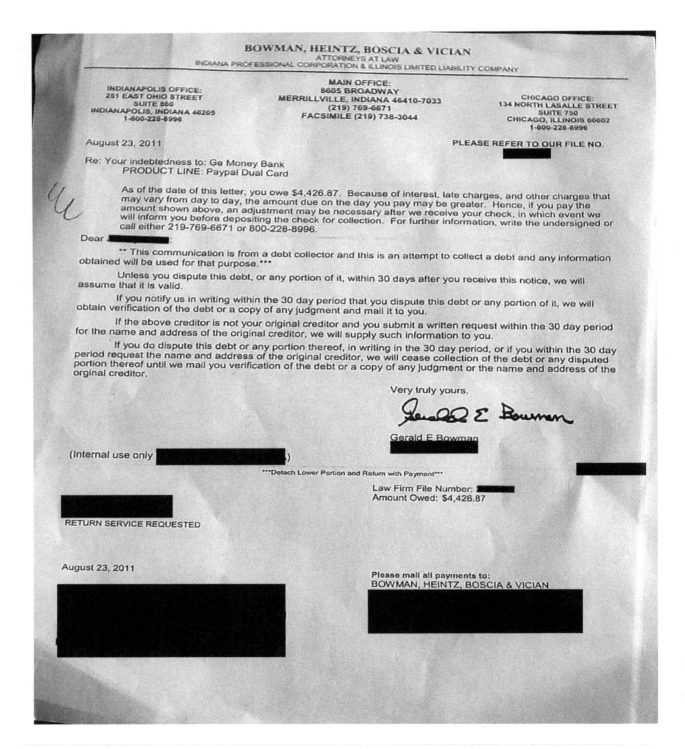

BOWMAN, HEINTZ, BOSCIA & VICIAN
ATTORNEYS AT LAW
INDIANA PROFESSIONAL CORPORATION & ILLINOIS LIMITED LIABILITY COMPANY

INDIANAPOLIS OFFICE:
251 EAST OHIO STREET
SUITE 860
INDIANAPOLIS, INDIANA 46205
1-800-228-8996

MAIN OFFICE:
8605 BROADWAY
MERRILLVILLE, INDIANA 46410-7033
(219) 769-6671
FACSIMILE (219) 738-3044

CHICAGO OFFICE:
134 NORTH LASALLE STREET
SUITE 750
CHICAGO, ILLINOIS 60602
1-800-228-8996

August 23, 2011

PLEASE REFER TO OUR FILE NO.

Re: Your indebtedness to: Ge Money Bank
    PRODUCT LINE: Paypal Dual Card

As of the date of this letter, you owe $4,426.87. Because of interest, late charges, and other charges that may vary from day to day, the amount due on the day you pay may be greater. Hence, if you pay the amount shown above, an adjustment may be necessary after we receive your check, in which event we will inform you before depositing the check for collection. For further information, write the undersigned or call either 219-769-6671 or 800-228-8996.

Dear J_____:

** This communication is from a debt collector and this is an attempt to collect a debt and any information obtained will be used for that purpose.***

Unless you dispute this debt, or any portion of it, within 30 days after you receive this notice, we will assume that it is valid.

If you notify us in writing within the 30 day period that you dispute this debt or any portion of it, we will obtain verification of the debt or a copy of any judgment and mail it to you.

If the above creditor is not your original creditor and you submit a written request within the 30 day period for the name and address of the original creditor, we will supply such information to you.

If you do dispute this debt or any portion thereof, in writing in the 30 day period, or if you within the 30 day period request the name and address of the original creditor, we will cease collection of the debt or any disputed portion thereof until we mail you verification of the debt or a copy of any judgment or the name and address of the orginal creditor.

Very truly yours,

Gerald E. Bowman (signature)

Gerald E. Bowman

(Internal use only _____)

Detach Lower Portion and Return with Payment

Law Firm File Number: ____
Amount Owed: $4,426.87

RETURN SERVICE REQUESTED

August 23, 2011

Please mail all payments to:
BOWMAN, HEINTZ, BOSCIA & VICIAN

And this isn't the first time this collection agency has gotten in trouble. Check out Justia.com for some more info.

Here are some of the results from http://dockets.justia.com for Bowman Heintz.

Cases filed matching "bowman heintz"

Cases 1 - 20 of 23 　　　　　　　　　○ RSS FEED 　　View as Table

LUKOVIC v. AMERICAN ACCEPTANCE COMPANY, L.L.C. et al

Filed: July 26, 2011 as 1:2011cv00995

Plaintiff: VESO LUKOVIC

Defendants: AMERICAN ACCEPTANCE COMPANY, L.L.C. and BOWMAN, HEINTZ, BOSCIA & VICIAN, P.C.

Presiding Judge: Jane Magnus-Stinson

Referring Judge: Debra McVicker Lynch

Cause Of Action: Fair Debt Collection Act

Court: Seventh Circuit > Indiana > Southern District Court

Type: Other Statutes > Other Statutory Actions

MCHALE v. NCO FINANCIAL SYSTEMS, INC. et al

Filed: July 26, 2011 as 1:2011cv00994

Plaintiff: BARBARA MCHALE

Defendants: BOWMAN, HEINTZ, BOSCIA & VICIAN, P.C. and NCO FINANCIAL SYSTEMS, INC.

Presiding Judge: Sarah Evans Barker

Referring Judge: Denise K. LaRue

Cause Of Action: Fair Debt Collection Act

Court: Seventh Circuit > Indiana > Southern District Court

Type: Other Statutes > Other Statutory Actions

Fick v. American Acceptance Company LLC et al

Filed: June 3, 2011 as 3:2011cv00229

Plaintiff: Heather Fick

Defendants: American Acceptance Company LLC and Bowman Heintz Boscia & Vician PC

Presiding Judge: James T Moody

Referring Judge: Christopher A Nuechterlein

Cause Of Action: Fair Debt Collection Act

Court: Seventh Circuit > Indiana > Northern District Court

Type: Other Statutes > Other Statutory Actions

If you scroll down, you will find this case.

COLLINS v. BOWMAN, HEINTZ, BOSCIA & VICIAN, P.C.

➕ Share | 🐦 Tweet | ☐ Like

Plaintiff:	ALINA C. COLLINS
Defendant:	BOWMAN, HEINTZ, BOSCIA & VICIAN, P.C.

Case Number:	1:2010cv01629
Filed:	December 16, 2010

Court:	Indiana Southern District Court
Office:	Indianapolis Office
Presiding Judge:	Jane Magnus-Stinson
Referring Judge:	Tim A. Baker

Nature of Suit:	Other Statutes - Other Statutory Actions
Cause:	15:1692 Fair Debt Collection Act
Jury Demanded By:	None

Access additional case information on PACER

Use the links below to access additional information about this case on the US Court's PACER system. A subscription to PACER is required.

Access this case on the Indiana Southern District Court's Electronic Court Filings (ECF) System

- Search for Party Aliases
- Associated Cases
- Attorneys
- Case File Location
- Case Summary
- Docket Report
- History/Documents
- Parties
- Related Transactions
- Check Status

It looks like Bowman was sued for violating the FDCPA. Let's find out more. You will need to register at Pacer.gov to view the case history. It will cost you a couple of cents to view each page from the court case, so you will need to give them your debit card number to keep on file. Definitely well worth the expense.

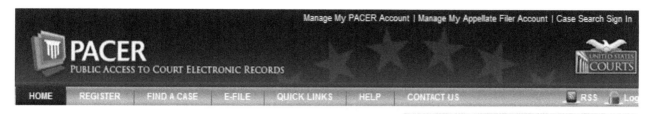

Public Access to Court Electronic Records (PACER) is an electronic public access service that allows users to obtain case and docket information from federal appellate, district and bankruptcy courts, and the PACER Case Locator via the Internet. PACER is provided by the federal Judiciary in keeping with its commitment to providing public access to court information via a centralized service.

WHAT'S NEW WITH PACER

- Free PACER Training Site (09/15/2011)
- Conference Approves Fee Increase (09/13/2011)
- Electronic Bankruptcy Noticing (08/08/2011)
- CM/ECF Release Notes (07/20/2011)
- New Remittance Address (03/01/2011)
- CM/ECF to Transition to PDF/A (10/29/2010)
- Digital Audio Recordings (05/11/2010)

More »

JUDICIARY ASSESSES PACER SERVICES

Judiciary announces the results of an independent assessment of PACER services. More

WHO CAN ACCESS PACER?

PACER is available to anyone who registers for an account.

The nearly one million PACER users include attorneys, pro se filers, government agencies, trustees, data collectors, researchers, educational and financial institutions, commercial enterprises, the media, and the general public.

FREQUENTLY USED

Court Links
Billing Information
Register for a PACER Account
Frequently Asked Questions
Manage My PACER Account
Manage My Appellate Filer Account
Case Search Sign In
Public Access Fee Schedule
October 2011 Newsletter
PACER Training Site

PACER CASE LOCATOR

The PACER Case Locator is a national index for U.S. District, Bankruptcy, and Appellate courts. A small subset of information from each case is transferred to the PACER Case Locator server each night. The system serves as a locator index for PACER. You may conduct nationwide searches to determine whether or not a party is involved in federal litigation.

Search Now

HOW DO I ACCESS PACER?

WHEN CAN I ACCESS PACER?

WHAT INFORMATION IS AVAILABLE ON PACER?

IS ALL CASE DATA AVAILABLE TO THE PUBLIC?

HOW MUCH DOES PACER COST?

WHAT IS CM/ECF?

HOW DO I GET MORE INFORMATION ABOUT PACER?

CONFERENCE APPROVES FEE INCREASE

In September 2011, the Judicial Conference of the United States authorized an increase in the Judiciary's electronic public access fee in response to increasing costs for maintaining and enhancing the electronic public access system. The increase in the electronic public access (EPA) fee, from $.08 to $.10 per page, will take effect on April 1, 2012. The change is needed to continue to support and improve the Public Access to Court Electronic Records (PACER) system, and to develop and implement the next generation of the Judiciary's Case Management/Electronic Case Filing system.

After you have registered with Pacer.gov, you can login and view the court documents. Click on the **Find a Case** link. Now click on the **Search the Pacer Case Locator** link. Now type in the case number, 1:2010cv01629, which you got from the Justia website.

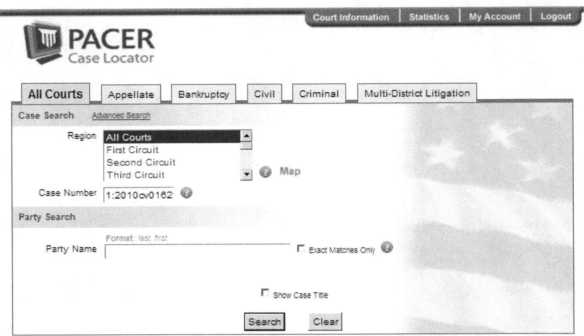

Now find the case with the plaintiff named Collins.

	Case Title	Court	Case	NOS	Date Filed	Date Closed
			Civil Results			
1	Smith v. Ploog Engineering Co., Inc.	caedce	1:2010-cv-01629	365	09/09/2010	10/05/2011
2	Tartan Partners Aviation, LLC v. Flight Options, LLC	codce	1:2010-cv-01629	190	07/09/2010	09/22/2010
3	UNITED STATES OF AMERICA v. ADOBE SYSTEMS, INC. et al	dodce	1:2010-cv-01629	410	09/24/2010	
4	Carter v. Gainey Corporation et al	gandce	1:2010-cv-01629	350	05/26/2010	06/14/2011
5	Evans v. Global Med-Net, Inc. et al	ilndce	1:2010-cv-01629	710	03/12/2010	11/01/2010
6	COLLINS v. BOWMAN, HEINTZ, BOSCIA & VICIAN, P.C.	insdce	1:2010-cv-01629	890	12/16/2010	03/23/2011
7	Dale v. Rapides Parish Sheriffs Office et al	lawdce	1:2010-cv-01629	440	10/26/2010	
8	Wymes et al v. Lustbader et al	mddce	1:2010-cv-01629	362	06/18/2010	
9	Masino et al v. Integrated Structures Corp.	nyedce	1:2010-cv-01629	791	04/13/2010	

The entire case is now at your fingertips.

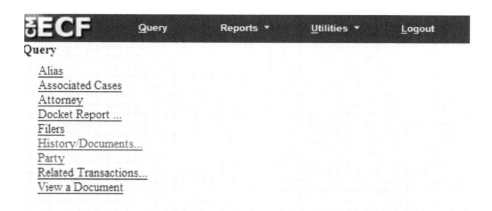

Let's check out the history of this case. Run the query.

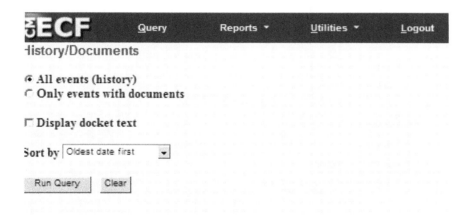

1:10-cv-01629-JMS-TAB COLLINS v. BOWMAN, HEINTZ, BOSCIA & VICIAN, P.C.
Jane Magnus-Stinson, presiding
Tim A. Baker, referral
Date filed: 12/16/2010
Date terminated: 03/23/2011
Date of last update: 09/14/2011

Here is the entire case. Remember it cost 8 cents per page to view each document.

History

Doc. No.	Dates	Description
1	Filed & Entered: 12/16/2010	Complaint
2	Filed & Entered: 12/16/2010	Civil Cover Sheet
3	Filed & Entered: 12/16/2010	Receipt
4	Filed & Entered: 12/16/2010	Summons Issued
5	Filed & Entered: 12/16/2010	Notice of Appearance
6	Filed & Entered: 12/16/2010	Magistrate Judge's Notice of Availability to Exercise Jurisdiction
7	Filed & Entered: 12/21/2010	Notice of Appearance
8	Filed & Entered: 12/29/2010	Magistrate Judge's Notice of Availability to Exercise Jurisdiction
9	Filed & Entered: 01/07/2011	NOTICE of Parties' First Extension of Time
10	Filed & Entered: 02/08/2011 Terminated: 02/09/2011	Motion for Continuance
11	Filed: 02/09/2011 Entered: 02/10/2011	Order on Motion for Continuance
12	Filed & Entered: 02/16/2011 Terminated: 03/23/2011	Motion to Dismiss
13	Filed & Entered: 02/16/2011	Brief/Memorandum in Support of Motion
14	Filed & Entered: 03/04/2011	Notice of Acceptance with Offer of Judgment
15	Filed & Entered: 03/17/2011	Submission
16	Filed & Entered: 03/23/2011	Closed Judgment
17	Filed & Entered: 04/06/2011 Terminated: 04/26/2011	Motion for Attorney Fees
18	Filed & Entered: 04/26/2011	Order on Motion for Attorney Fees
19	Filed & Entered: 06/17/2011 Terminated: 06/23/2011	Motion for Proceedings Supplemental
20	Filed & Entered: 06/23/2011	Order on Motion for Proceedings Supplemental
21	Filed: 08/03/2011 Entered: 08/04/2011	Proceedings Supplemental
22	Filed & Entered: 08/19/2011 Terminated: 09/01/2011	Motion for Attorney Fees
23	Filed & Entered: 08/25/2011 Terminated: 08/25/2011	Motion to Vacate

24	Filed & Entered:	08/25/2011	Order on Motion to Vacate
25	Filed & Entered:	08/26/2011	Certificate of Service
26	Filed & Entered: Terminated:	08/30/2011 09/01/2011	Motion to Withdraw
27	Filed & Entered:	09/01/2011	Order on Motion for Attorney Fees
28	Filed & Entered: Terminated:	09/10/2011 09/14/2011	Motion (Other)
29	Filed & Entered:	09/10/2011	Motion (Other)
30	Filed & Entered:	09/10/2011	Affidavit
31	Filed & Entered:	09/12/2011	Certificate of Service
32	Filed & Entered:	09/12/2011	Certificate of Service
33	Filed & Entered:	09/12/2011	Certificate of Service
34	Filed & Entered:	09/14/2011	Scheduling Order

PACER Service Center			
Transaction Receipt			
10/09/2011 17:32:33			
PACER Login:	ts4893	Client Code:	
Description:	History/Documents	Search Criteria:	1:10-cv-01629-JMS-TAB
Billable Pages:	1	Cost:	0.08

V. STATEMENT OF FACTS

6. Defendant filed a lawsuit on an alleged debt against Plaintiff on November 9, 2009 in Marion County – Center Township Small Claims Court, Cause No. 49K01-0911-SC-11954 (hereinafter "state court lawsuit").

7. At some time prior to December 17, 2009, Defendant prepared a document titled "INFORMATION SHEET" (attached hereto as Exhibit A).

8. At some time prior to December 17, 2009, Defendant enlisted the staff of the Marion County – Center Township Small Claims Court to distribute to defendants that had been sued by Defendant in the Marion County – Center Township Small Claims Court and to collect it after it had been filled out.

9. On December 17, 2009, Plaintiff attended court on the state court lawsuit. Plaintiff was given the INFORMATION SHEET by court staff upon arriving at the court. Plaintiff asked the court staff person who gave her the form if she was required to complete it. The court staff person replied "Yes."

10. On May 13, 2010, Plaintiff attended court on the state court lawsuit. Plaintiff was given the INFORMATION SHEET by court staff upon arriving at the court.

A. Fair Debt Collection Practices Act

11. Plaintiff repeats, re-alleges and incorporates by reference paragraphs one through ten above.

12. By having court staff distribute the INFORMATION SHEET to Plaintiff, Defendant violated the Fair Debt Collection Practices Act. These violations include, but are not limited to:

    (a) The false representation or implication that Defendant is vouched for or affiliated with the state court, in violation of 15 U.S.C. § 1692e(1);

    (b) The use and distribution of a written communication which simulates or is falsely represented to be a document authorized, issued or approved by the state court and which creates a false impression as to its source, authorization or approval, in violation of 15 U.S.C. § 1692e(9);

    (c) The use of any false representation or deceptive means to collect or attempt to collect a debt and to obtain information concerning a consumer, in violation of 15 U.S.C. § 1692e(10);

    (d) The false representation or implication that a document is legal process, in violation of 15 U.S.C. § 1692e(13).

If you look at the summons, Bowman Heintz violated the FDCPA by misrepresenting certain documents given to the plaintiff that were in fact not authorized or approved by the Indiana state court. Below is what the plaintiff wants from Bowman Heintz.

13. As a result of the violations of the Fair Debt Collection Practices Act, Defendant is liable to Plaintiff for her actual damages, statutory damages, punitive damages, costs, attorney fees and all other appropriate relief.

WHEREFORE, Plaintiff Alina C. Collins respectfully requests that the Court enter judgment in her favor and against Defendant in an amount that will compensate her for her actual damages, statutory damages, punitive damages, costs, attorney fees and all other appropriate relief.

Below is the summons.

UNITED STATES DISTRICT COURT
for the
Southern District of Indiana

ALINA C. COLLINS	)
Plaintiff	)
v.	) Civil Action No.
BOWMAN, HEINTZ, BOSCIA & VICIAN P.C.	)
Defendant	)

1:10-cv-1229ms -TAB

SUMMONS IN A CIVIL ACTION

To: *(Defendant's name and address)* Bowman, Heintz, Boscia & Vician, P.C.
c/o Gerald E. Bowman
8605 Broadway
Merrillville, IN 46410

A lawsuit has been filed against you.

Within 20 days after service of this summons on you (not counting the day you received it) — or 60 days if you are the United States or a United States agency, or an officer or employee of the United States described in Fed. R. Civ. P. 12 (a)(2) or (3) — you must serve on the plaintiff an answer to the attached complaint or a motion under Rule 12 of the Federal Rules of Civil Procedure. The answer or motion must be served on the plaintiff or plaintiff's attorney, whose name and address are: Robert E. Duff
Indiana Consumer Law Group/The Law Office of Robert E. Duff
380 Mount Zion Road, Suite C
Lebanon, IN 46052

If you fail to respond, judgment by default will be entered against you for the relief demanded in the complaint. You also must file your answer or motion with the court.

CLERK OF COURT   CLERK

Date: **DEC 16 2010**

Signature of Clerk or Deputy Clerk

Now takre a look at the judgement. Looks like Bowman Heintz not only lost, but they also owe several thousand dollars to the plaintiff.

ALINA C. COLLINS, Plaintiff, v. BOWMAN, HEINTZ, BOSCIA & VICIAN P.C., Defendant.	CASE NO. 1:10-CV-1629 JMS-TAB

JUDGMENT

Pursuant to Plaintiff's acceptance of Defendant's Offer of Judgment, and Federal Rule of Civil Procedure 68(a), the Clerk of Court hereby enters judgment in favor of Plaintiff in the amount of $1,001.00, plus attorney fees and costs. Plaintiff is hereby directed to submit a petition for attorney fees and costs within fourteen days of this Judgment.

03/23/2011

Here is another document which states the defendant agreed to pay over $8000 to the plaintiff.

> Please be advised that if the check ($8127.98) is not received by this Friday, September 9, I will request a new hearing date, file a motion to enforce our settlement, re-file my motion for attorney fees and will not agree to cancel the new hearing date.

21. Defendant has not yet paid the judgment, nor the amount it agreed to pay.

22. Since the agreement was reached wherein Defendant agreed to pay $8,127.98 in full satisfaction of the judgment in this case, Plaintiff has incurred additional attorney fees in the amount of $810 to date in attempting to collect on the agreement and filing this motion and requesting the court to reset the hearing in this matter.

23. The foregoing time was reasonable and necessary in attempting to collect the judgment in this matter.

24. I anticipate incurring an additional 3.3 hours in preparing for and attending the

Remember, these court documents (which you now have complete acess to thanks to Justia.com and Pacer.gov) give you valuable information about collection agencies that spend time in court. You can now find out what law firms they use, what laws they violate, and how successful they are in court. Plus, these documents will also give you specific court cases to reference in your validation letters, cases that involve the very same collection agencies that are coming after you. These scumbags will be less likely to sue you if you know about every court case that they lost, and know how to sue them for thousands of dollars. Knowledge is power!

WRITING THE VALIDATION LETTER

Now it's time to make the collection agencies go away. Most of the time it can be done in two simple steps. Both involve letters that you write. Here is exactly how it is done.

First, you will get a collection letter in the mail. If you get a phone call first, tell them nothing except that you need to see everything in writing. Tell them to send you a letter and hang up. Don't admit to owing money to anyone. Remember, you do not have sufficient knowledge of any debt. The burden of proof is on the collection agency and original creditor. Below is a collection letter received from SRA Associates, Inc. They claim that they were hired by Dell Financial Services, and that $5745.62 is owed.

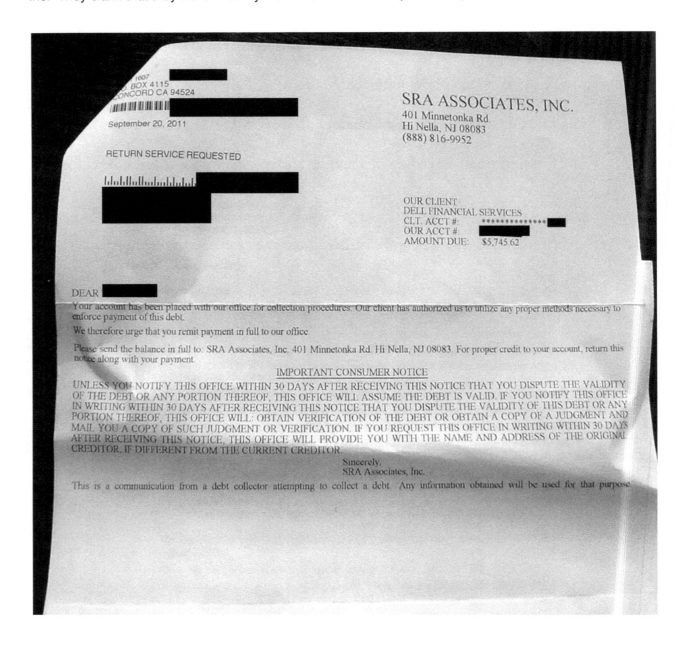

STEP 1. Do your research. Google the company and find out what complaints they are getting. Find out if they are really a law firm. Find out what their game plan is from other consumers. Ripoffreport.com and pissedconsumer.com are some great websites to check out when doing your research. Also, be sure to call up the original creditor and ask them for a copy of the original signed contract. See if it even exists anymore.

Google   sra associates inc

Advanced search

Search   About 4,440,000 results (0.16 seconds)

Everything

Images

Maps

Videos

News

Shopping

More

Carmel, IN
Change location

Show search tools

SRA Associates
www.sraassociates.com/
SRA Associates is a nationally licensed and bonded receivables management services organization located in Southern New Jersey. Founded in 1994, SRA ...
Contact Us - Employment - Services - People

401 Minnetonka Road   Bus: Rt-30 at Columbia Ave
Hi-Nella, NJ 08084
(856) 755-0500
Directions - Is this accurate?

Place page
pissedconsumer.com (5)

SRA Associates - Contact Us
www.sraassociates.com/?d=292.4983
Apr 3, 2009 – **SRA Associates Inc**. 401 Minnetonka Road Hi-Nella, New Jersey ...

✛ Show more results from sraassociates.com

SRA Associates Inc. Business Review in Hi Nella, NJ - New Jersey ...
www.bbb.org/new-jersey/.../sra-associates-in-hi-nella-nj-26001703
Jan 25, 2011 – BBB's Business Review for **SRA Associates Inc**., Business Reviews and Ratings for **SRA Associates Inc**. in Hi Nella, NJ.

SRA Associates @ Pissed Consumer
sra-associates.pissedconsumer.com/
SRA Associates, Inc. is a receivables management services organization. The company is headquartered in Hi-Nella, New Jersey. SRA Associates was founded ...

SRA Associates Inc., Hi-Nella (Somerdale), New Jersey Complaint...
www.complaintsboard.com/panel.php?action=profile...
Jun 13, 2008 – **SRA Associates Inc**., Hi-Nella (Somerdale), New Jersey Complaints, Reviews: Telephone harassment. Collections Agencies.

SRA Associates Inc â€¹ My account has been sold to them. What to ...
www.debtconsolidationcare.com/forums/sra-assoc.html
Dec 19, 2005 – **SRA Associates Inc** is a New Jersey based licensed collection agency, who may purchase your account. Read to know more about what you ...

SRA Associates, Inc. | Collection Agency | Free Collection Agencies ...

Post By	SRA Associates Reviews	Hits
Anonymous	**SRA Associates** - SRA calls a wrong number and person day and night to harrass me. This is a deadbeat company with people who do not listen and could not find there *** with both hands. They have been calling every phone number we have listed in search of someone... #233296 Apr 20, 2011	392
Anonymous	**SRA Associates** - SRA harassment SRA, a debt collection agency, continues to harass us over a 5 year old claim against our son who moved out years ago. He signed for a girlfriend to purchase a new car. His credit ... #202670 Oct 14, 2010	500
	Self-Publish Your Book Get Help from Start to Finish + 555 Free Book Promotion Tips Now www.createspace.com **Low Cost Life Insurance** We Give Personalized Quotes That Fit Your Budget; In Just 24 Hours! www.SelectQuote.com AdChoices ▷	
Damienbu...	**SRA Associates** - Violation of SCRA 50 U.S.C App 527 SRA Associates just recently called me and informed my wife that my SCRA porotection ended in 2/2010. However under Title 10 orders as an Activated Reservist until I get off Titl... #182181 May 15, 2010	992
Lexerot	**SRA Associates** - You've Got The Wrong Number! All day long I get calls from these people. Every day I can expect several automated calls. I wouldn't be as pissed if they were actually looking for me. They are ca... #172865 Feb 27, 2010	814
MrsWhite...	**SRA Associates** - Settlement Letters are not Law Abinding I have been speaking to a collection representative on behalf of my husband's account. I've informed the collector that I am also a collector and have been for over 10 year... #169797 Feb 02, 2010	1123
	SRA Associates harassment calls SRA Associates started with phone calls to my elderly uncle last year. He doesn't owe anybody any money. Last year, he was smart enough to keep a record of each phone	1692

STEP 2. Write the validation letter.
Validation requires the collector to identify who owes the debt to whom. That's about it. So they have to take some time to gather up a few billing statements and mail them out to the debtor. And during that time they can't try to collect on the debt or file a lawsuit against you. However, just because they can validate a debt, doesn't mean you should accept it. Validating a debt does not mean you can legally prove a debt in court. So basically it is just part of the game that lets bill collectors know that you are willing to fight. On the other hand, there are some collectors or junk debt buyers that will not even be able to get their hands on a few billing statements, so they will not be able to validate anything, and therefore, will have no legal authority to sue you. If you don't request validation, then the debt can be deemed admissible in court.

So send out the validation letter right away. The quicker, the better. You can download the letter I wrote, and use it to stop the collection agencies that are coming after you.

You can download the template here:

http://snotboards.com/sra_example1.zip

Save the zip file to your desktop, then open up the Microsoft Word 2007 (.docx) document. Be sure to change the creditor and personal information so it reflects your situation. If you need a zip program, they are free at Adobe.com.

So here is an example of the first debt validation letter that you will send to the collection agency.

1/09/2012

Name
ADDRESS
City, State Zip

Re: Citibank, N.A.
Account #: XXXXXXXXXXXXX18
Reference #: Citi Mastercard

Dear NCO Financial Systems, Inc:

I am writing in response to a notice I received on 1/09/12 from NCO Financial Systems, Inc. In accordance to the FDCPA, I am requesting a validation of this debt from your company, which should include the following:

(1) The amount of the debt and the name of the creditor to whom the debt is owed;

(2) Legal proof that you are licensed to collect debts in Indiana on behalf of this creditor, and legal proof that you have procured a bond in the State of Indiana as required per Article 11 of Title 25 of the Indiana Code;

(3) Complete payment history of this debt from the original creditor, including all interest and fees properly itemized, which was established in the case of *Fields v. Wilber Law Firm, Donald L. Wilber and Kenneth Wilber, USCA-02-C-0072, 7th Circuit Court, Sept 2004. (Note: According to the Federal Trade Commission Wollman Opinion, computer printouts do not constitute proper debt validation;*

(4) A copy of the instrument, or signed agreement between myself and Citibank, which is required under Indiana Trial Rule 9.2. *(Note: An Affidavit of Debt will not be accepted as proper validation and will be challenged with a Sworn Denial, which was demonstrated in Todd v. Weltman, Weinberg & Reis Co., L.P.A., 434 F.3d 432 (6th Cir. 2006).* Moreover, mailing a fraudulent affidavit is a violation US CODE TITLE 18 CHAPTER 63, which is a felony that carries penalties ranging from up to 10 years in prison and $1000,000.00 in fines;

(5) Copies of all term change notices, which are required for every change Citibank made to the original contract;

(6) A copy of the assignment, or legal agreement between NCO and Citibank, which includes the real damages, or actual amount paid for the alleged debt, and all other fees properly itemized;

Here is page 2.

(7) Note: If there is an underlying arbitration clause associated with this claim, I hereby exercise it, and waive your litigation rights to this claim, per the arbitration clause.

I am disputing this debt; therefore, until validated your information concerning this debt is inaccurate. Thus, if you have already reported this debt to any credit-reporting agency (CRA) or Credit Bureau (CB) then, you must immediately inform them of my dispute with this debt. Reporting information that you know to be inaccurate, or failing to report information correctly violates the Fair Credit Reporting Act § 1681s-2. Should you pursue a judgment without validating this debt, I will inform the judge and request the case be dismissed based on your failure to comply with the FDCPA. If your office fails to respond to this request within 30 days, this will be construed as a waiver of your claims against me.

Sincerely

Your Name
I

Let's discuss the validation letter point by point.

(1) This is how much money you owe to the original creditor (OC). Keep in mind that the amount that you owe to the original credit cannot change unless specified on the original contract you signed. So collection agencies or lawyers can't add on extra fees unless your contract said so. Without seeing the original signed contract, the collector can't add on any extra fees. If you end up in court, the collection agency would have to sue your for additional fees that are deemed reasonable if allowed in the original contract. Some collection agencies will break the law and actually double the amount that you owe to the OC, and unfortunately some people will pay them that amount. So check this number with your last statement from the OC. It could present a good defense if they can prove you do actually owe the debt. If you owe $2000, they can't sue you for $2001.

You are also asking for the name of the original creditor. If your debt gets sold to several other junk debt buyers, the contract that you signed with the original creditor determines how much you legally might owe.

(2) Legal proof that a collection agency is licensed and bonded in your state. Some states require this for some, or all of a company's collection efforts. If so, list the actual state code. In my case, a collection company or law firm has to be from my state to sue me. They can use standard interstate collection practices like the phone, fax, mail, and email if they are outside of my state. This means a debt collector has to hire a local law firm or if they want to sue me. Here is a good website that describes each state's collection agency laws.

http://collectionagency.lifetips.com/cat/60040/about-state-by-state-debt-recovery/index.html

Note: if you live in a state like California that does not require licensing or bonding, then you can leave section 3 off of your validation letter.

(3) Complete payment history. The burden of proof is on the original creditor, or whoever owns the debt to produce evidence of every single charge that was made. So they need to keep records that go back many years. Often, the original creditor doesn't keep these records, which is a big mistake on their part. In the case of Fields vs. Wilber Law Firm, the decision stated that the debt collector must get billing statements from the original creditor in order to come up with the exact amount owed. A collector cannot just come up with a piece of paper with some numbers on it. And in some courts, copies of the actual billing statements are required, not account summary print offs, re-prints, or computer generated files

that are made **after the fact**. A legal copy of a billing statement should be a graphic file, like a JPEG, TIFF or GIFF file. The payment history should look exactly like the bills you received on a monthly basis, just printed on white copy paper. Compare a copy that the debt collector sends you with an old bill that you have. How are they different? In other words, the billing statements the collection agency sends you from the original creditor need to be accurate copies of your billing statements from the original creditor. The debt collector can't just make one up on their computer. Although this is backed up by a Federal Trade Commission opinion letter, you never know whether a judge will deem computer printouts admissible or not. Check with your local district courts in your state to see if they have any opinions on debt validation. Check out the "copies" of similar billing statements that two different collection agencies sent me as validation. One has logos on it, and the other doesn't. If this ended up in court, you would seek out the identity of the person who obtained this copy (through discovery), and how he obtained it and authenticated it.

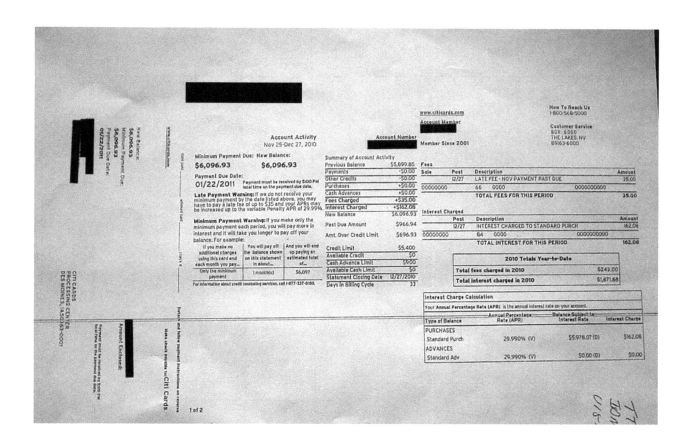

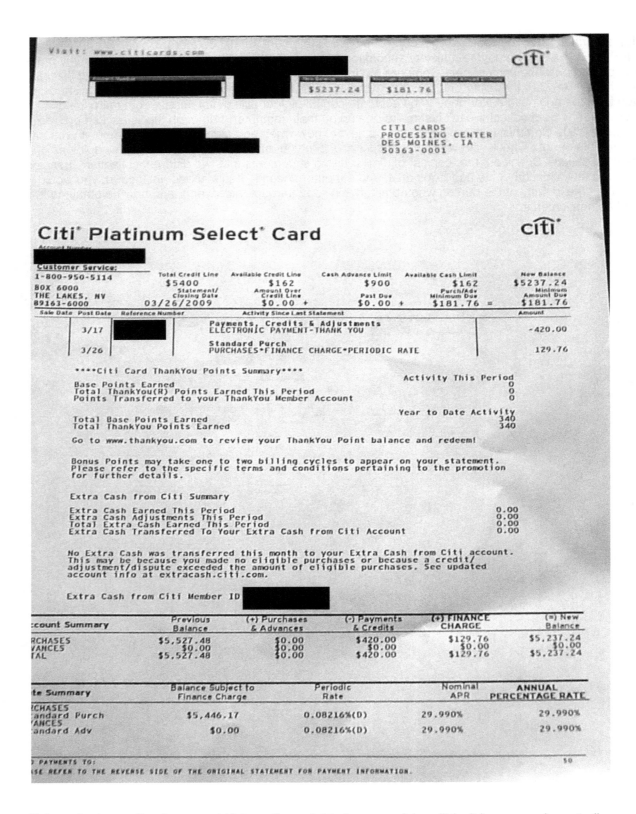

If the collector can't get payment history, they might also use a fake affidavit by a records custodian (affiant), which is hearsay, unless it is an affidavit from the original creditor. And if it is from the OC, then chances are it is also fraudulent. That is where the Sworn Denial comes in handy when the collector tries to take you to court. That means the records custodian from the original credit has to come to your town to testify in person. That is by no means cheap or easy to do, especially if the debt is old. An account expert should have your original contract, plus records of all purchases including signatures for those purchases. They have to prove two things: you opened the account and you used the card. If you applied over the phone, a recording of the over the phone agreement should be brought to court. Your original agreement probably stated that use of the credit card is proof of a contract. But you still need proof. Show me those words on the original signed contract.

(4) A copy of the signed contract. This is basic contract law. Without a signed contract, there is not sufficient proof of debt if the collector is suing for breach of contract. The debt collectors usually never get this, so they must rely on an Affidavit of Debt, which you can attack with a Motion to Dismiss, Motion to Strike, Discovery, or Sworn Denial. If the collector has not given you proof of any debt, you don't have to pay it. The Todd vs. Weltman, Weinberg & Reis case determined in a federal court that a debt collector cannot submit a false affidavit.

Here are some more important cases regarding Affidavits of Debt. This info comes from the website:

http://www.creditinfocenter.com/legal/motion-to-strike-affidavit.shtml

List of Cases Where Affidavits were Determined to be False or Fraudulent

Debt buyers regularly submit affidavits which purport to be made on personal knowledge but in fact are based on reading a computer screen.

- Luke v. Unifund CCR Partners, No. 2-06-444-CV, 2007 Tex.App. LEXIS' 7096 (2nd Dist. Ft. Worth Aug. 31, 2007).
- Palisades Collection, LLC a/p/o AT&T Wireless v. Gonzalez, 10 Misc. 3d 1058A; 809 N.Y.S.2d 482 (N.Y.County Civ. Ct. 2005):
  Todd v. Weltman, Weinberg & Reis Co., L.P.A., 434 F.3d 432 (6th Cir. 2006);
- Delawder v. Platinum Financial, 443 F. Supp. 2d 942 (S.D.Ohio March 1,2005);
- Griffith v. Javitch, Block & Rathbone, LLP, 1:04cv238 (S.D.Ohio, July 8, 2004);
- Gionis v. Javitch, Block & Rathbone, 405 F. Supp. 2d 856 (S.D.Ohio. 2005);
- Blevins v. Hudson & Keyse, Inc., 395 F. Supp. 2d 655 (S.D.Ohio 2004), later opinion, 395 F.Supp.2d 662 (S.D.Ohio 2004);
- Stolicker v. Muller, Muller, Richmond, Harms, Meyers & Sgroi, P.C., 1:04cv733 (W.D.Mich., Sept. 8, 2005).

For example in *Palisades Collection, LLC a/p/o AT&T Wireless v. Gonzalez, 10 Misc. 3d 1058A; 809 N.Y.S.2d 482 (N.Y.County Civ. Ct. 2005)*, an affidavit was submitted from a Ms. Bergman who claimed to be Vice President of Palisades and familiar with business record-keeping practices. Being familiar with records in the course of doing business is one way debt collectors can side-step the hearsay exception:

(5) Copies of all term changes. These contract modifications are changes to the original contract, like a change in interest rate. Some contracts require your signature for all changes to the original agreement. If the debt collector can't get the original contract, then there is no way to justify the 29% interest rate for not paying your bills to the original creditor. The contract has to give the OC the right to modify the terms, which most do. So this is just more paperwork and headache for the debt collector. Odds are they will ignore this, if not all of your validation requests. But it lets them know you are ready to throw the kitchen sink at them if needed. You are not an easy victim.

(6) A copy of the deal between the OC and the junk debt buyer, or collection agency. They have to legally prove that they own the debt, otherwise they have legal standing to take you to court. Debt collectors do, however, fraudulently sue people all the time. But if you show up to court, they usually can't win. The OC or collection agency will often hire local lawyers if they need to sue you.

(7) Requesting arbitration. This is a way to settle disputes without going to court, and most credit card agreements have an arbitration clause in them. This is a useful tool that is used to prevent class action lawsuits and bad publicity; however, it can be a disaster if the tables are turned, and the collection

agency is trying to sue the consumer. The problem is the cost for the plaintiff. It will cost the bill collector several thousand dollars for arbitration, so it is not worth the time and trouble unless you owe a bunch of money. In other words, mention "arbitration" and you far less likely to be sued, especially if you only owe a few thousand dollars.

If the collector agrees to arbitrate, you can find the necessary paperwork and info at the Judicial Arbitration and Mediation Service (JAMS)(www.jamsadr.com) or the American Arbitration Association (AAA)(www.adr.org). You should also get a "Notice of Intent to Initiate Arbitration" in the mail. The cost will be around $250 for you and several thousand dollars for the creditor.

Check your credit card arbitration clause. Take a look at some of the common credit card agreements below. You are going to want to find the agreement closest to the date that you defaulted. Then you will need to look for the arbitration clause. Credit card companies are now removing the arbitration clause, so it is important to see if arbitration is possible. Of course, if the debt collector can't get a copy of the original contract, then they may just assume that an arbitration clause exists.

http://teh402.blogspot.com
http://www.federalreserve.gov/creditcardagreements/
http://www.creditcards.com/credit-card-news/credit-card-agreements-1282.php#agreements

The last paragraph in the debt validation letter lets the collector know that you are disputing the debt, and the laws that go along with that.

STEP 3. Ship it out. Get a shipping account at usps.com right away. You will have to use
your debit card to register. I use priority mail with a signature when I ship to bill collectors. Other people like to use registered mail with a return receipt. Priority mail is quick and easy to do online, the shipping is fast, and you can order the cardboard priority mail envelopes for free. After you have an account, just click on **ship a package**, enter the addresses, print out the postage, tape it to your envelope, and stick the priority mail envelope in your mailbox. Shipping should cost around $8 for priority mail plus a signature. Remember, you have to get a signature! This is your only proof that the collectors received the debt validation request. Plus, you can get this proof emailed to you after it has been delivered.

Get an account at USPS right away. Otherwise you will end up spending lots of time at the post office.

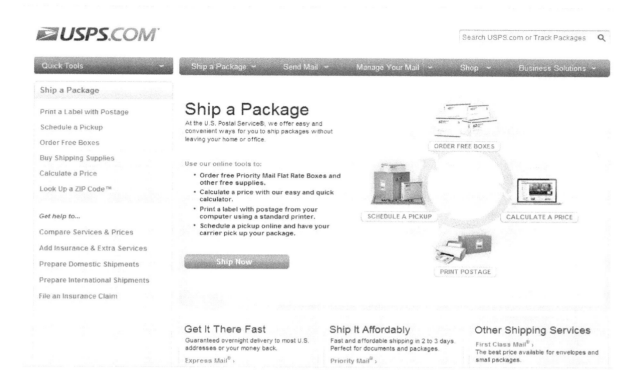

Order plenty of priority 12.5" x 9.5" mail envelopes right now. You will need them soon.

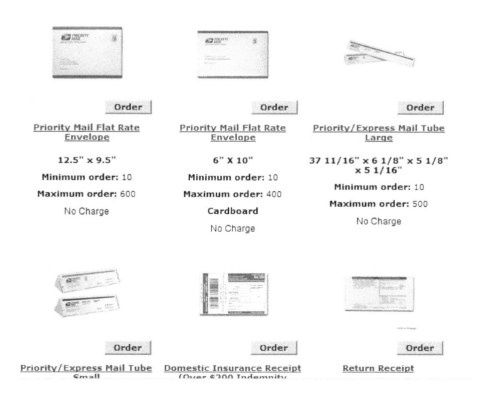

Order	Order	Order
Priority Mail Flat Rate Envelope	**Priority Mail Flat Rate Envelope**	**Priority/Express Mail Tube Large**
12.5" x 9.5"	6" X 10"	37 11/16" x 6 1/8" x 5 1/8" x 5 1/16"
Minimum order: 10	Minimum order: 10	Minimum order: 10
Maximum order: 600	Maximum order: 400	Maximum order: 500
No Charge	Cardboard	No Charge
	No Charge	

Order	Order	Order
Priority/Express Mail Tube Small	**Domestic Insurance Receipt (Over $200 Indemnity**	**Return Receipt**

Next, print out a shipping label.

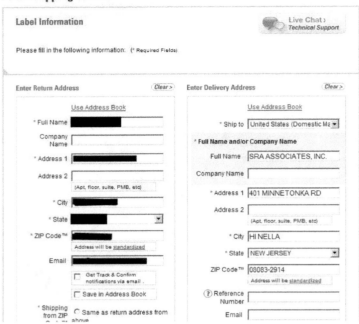

Use priority mail with a signature.

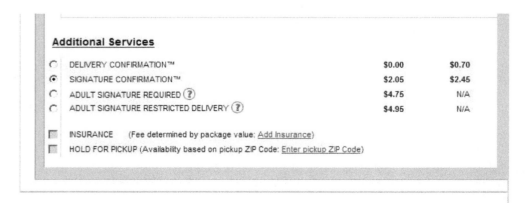

Print Shipping Labels

Print Label

Live Chat ›
Technical Support

Label Options

☐ Print without Receipt and Shipping Instructions. ⑦

Your Agreement

* ☑ I agree that I will present any items that are liquid, perishable or potentially hazardous to a postal employee for acceptance and that all fragile items are properly packaged. ⑦ Any item containing cigarette and smokeless tobacco must be presented to a Postal employee at a Retail Post Office location for proper induction. ⑦

Print Sample Label   (Pay and Print)

Printing Instructions:

- Adobe® Reader® Version 5 or higher is required to print your label(s).
  Download Adobe® Reader®

- Labels will print to your computer's default printer.

- To test your printer: Print a Sample Label

Here is the label printed out on copy paper. Save the bottom section with the tracking number.

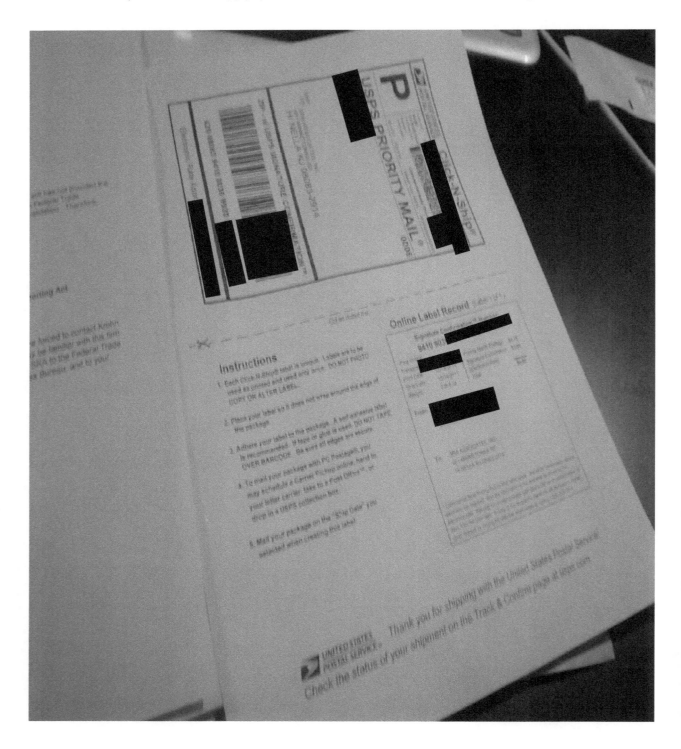

Keep this for your records. Now ship it.

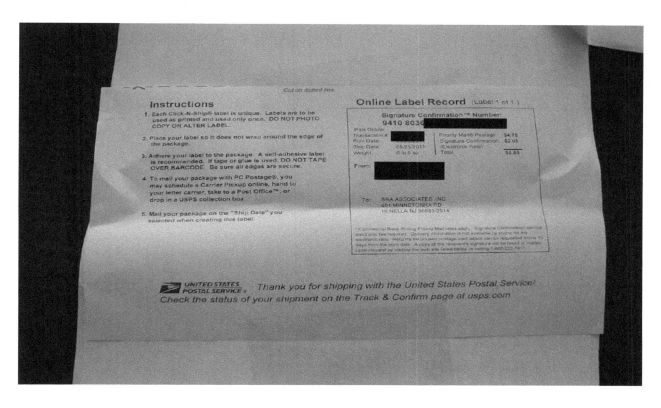

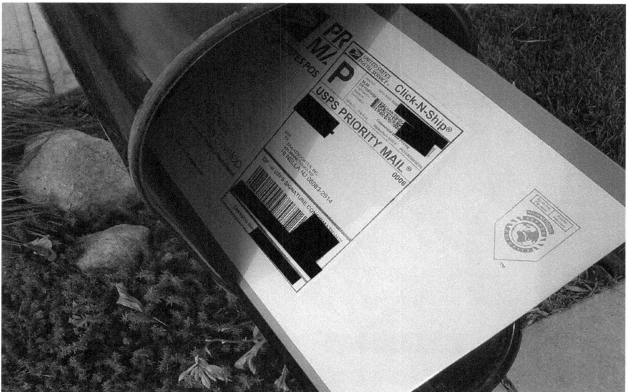

You can track the package at USPS.com. Click on the request proof of delivery link for a copy of the collection agency's signature. Now you have proof they received the letter.

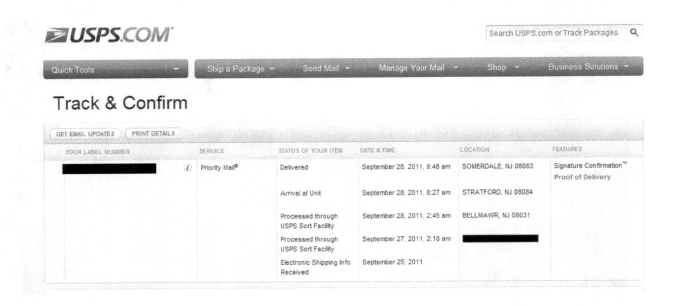

Here is an email that you will get when the letter has been delivered.

███████████ has requested that you receive a Track & Confirm update, as shown below.

Track & Confirm e-mail update information provided by the U.S. Postal Service.

Label Number ███████████████

Service Type: Priority Mail Signature Confirmation

Shipment Activity	Location	Date & Time
Delivered	SOMERDALE NJ 08083	10/17/11 9:46am
Out for Delivery	STRATFORD NJ 08084	10/17/11 8:57am
Sorting Complete	STRATFORD NJ 08084	10/17/11 8:47am
Arrival at Unit	STRATFORD NJ 08084	10/17/11 8:33am
Processed through USPS Sort Facility	BELLMAWR NJ 08031	10/17/11 1:50am
Processed through USPS Sort Facility	███████████████	10/15/11 9:22pm

Here is the proof that was requested. Keep this with your records.

UNITED STATES
POSTAL SERVICE.

Date: 10/20/2011

█████████████

The following is in response to your 10/20/2011 request for delivery information on your Signature Confirmation(TM) item number ███████████████████ The delivery record shows that this item was delivered on 09/28/2011 at 09:48 AM in SOMERDALE, NJ 08083 to J GAYNOR. The scanned image of the recipient information is provided below.

Signature of Recipient:

STEP 4. Wait about a month. After 30 days or so, you will probably get a package in the mail. The collection agency will send you some computer generated statements from the past year or so, and hope you are dumb enough to accept it as solid evidence. Unless you have a copy of the actual contract you signed, then you must move on to the next step. Note: if they do produce a copy of the original signed contract and all of your billing statements, then call up the original creditor and make a deal for 50% of what you owe, separated into 3-4 payments. Finding the actual contract is very rare, especially since many credit card offers are accepted over the phone without a contract. But if they have everything they need to win a court case, then you are not left with many options. If you can't afford to make a deal, then you will have to play hardball and buy some time. File complaints with the Federal Trade Commission, State Attorney General where the collection agency is located, and the Better Business Bureau where the collection agency is located. Normally you can find some type of violation in the collection letters they send out. Debt collection letters cannot be misleading in any way. And unfortunately, most of them are. The collection letters have to be easy to understand to the least sophisticated consumer. The case of Sparkman v. Zwicker & Assocs., P.C made this clear. I will explain more about filing complaints later on in this book.

On the next page you will see the next letter received from SRA Associates, and the package they sent. The package included a few copies of some billing statements, and a few receipts of purchases they claimed was made. There was no complete billing history, no copy of the original contract, no proof that they are allowed to collect in the debtor's state, and no proof that they even work for Dell. There is really no proof that this company or the debt is legit. So it's time to move on to the next step.

STEP 5. Send the threatening letter. Now it is basically time to tell the collection agency to go rot in hell. Here is where the laws are in your favor. Since the collector has not properly validated the debt, any more communication will be a violation of the FDCPA. A debt collector simply cannot keep harassing you if he can't prove you owe them any money. So it is put up or shut up time. Either they take you to court without evidence, or they simply go away. So far I have found that 100% of the time they simply give up and force the original creditor to hire someone else who is a little more sleezier and reckless. The debt collector knows they are not going to get any money out of you at this point, and they know that you are aware they can't get the original contract. And they also know that you firmly believe an affidavit won't work. And even if they did somehow win, there is also an appeals process, which could take years. It's much easier to go after someone who doesn't know the rules of the game. Remember, original creditors and collection agencies simply cannot sue everyone. Think of it like this. You are on a camping trip and a hungry bear is about to attack. All you have to do is be just a little bit quicker than the slowest person at the campground. Animals attack the weak. They usually don't go after the strong.

Here is the package of junk SRA sent.

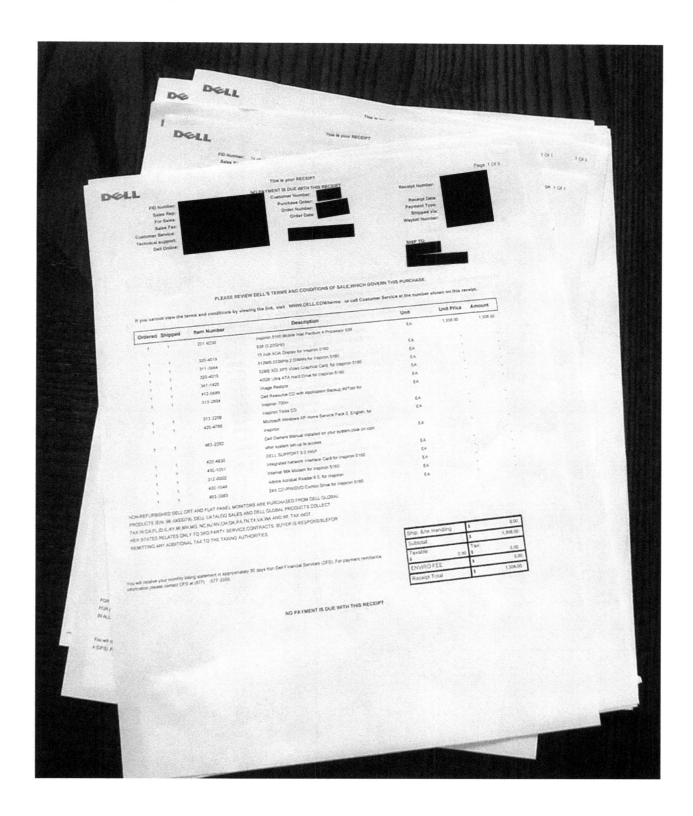

Here is the threatening letter. You might notice that a case number and law firm name was added to the letter below. Most debt collectors have been sued in the states they do business in. And if you are going to make threats, you might as well make real ones. You could contact this lawyer if you get sued because they charge a very fair flat fee, and already know how to fight NCO. On the next, page I will show you how to get some local litigation to add to your second validation letter. You can download the template for it here: http://www.snotboards.com/validation2.zip

Re: Citibank, N.A.
Account #: ██████████
Reference #: ██████████

Dear NCO Financial Systems, Inc:

I am writing in response to computer printouts received from NCO Financial Systems, Inc. on 1/26/12. NCO has still not provided the proper debt validation or a valid assignment of debt from Citibank. According to the Federal Trade Commission Wollman Opinion, computer generated forms made to look like billing statements from the original creditor are not sufficient for debt validation. The Federal Trade Commission has made it clear that a "mere itemization" is not sufficient proof to validate a debt. NCO has also failed to provide the name, job title, and phone number of the individual who authenticated these printouts.

Therefore, the FDCPA states:

1. NCO Financial Systems, Inc. is not allowed to collect the alleged debt,

2. NCO Financial Systems, Inc. is not allowed to contact me about the debt, and

3. NCO Financial Systems, Inc. is not allowed to report it under the Fair Credit Reporting Act.

If you continue to demonstrate willful noncompliance [15 U.S.C. § 1681n], I will be forced to contact the law offices of Steven J. Halbert and take legal action against you in my local district court. You may be familiar with his firm in the case Merski v. NCO Financial Systems, Inc. (1:2011cv01309). I will also report NCO to the Federal Trade Commission, Pennsylvania Attorney General Linda Kelly, the Better Business Bureau, and to your client, Citibank.

Sincerely,

If you want to add a case to your second validation request, here is how you do it. First, go to http://dockets.justia.com/ and type in the name of the collection agency that has contacted you.

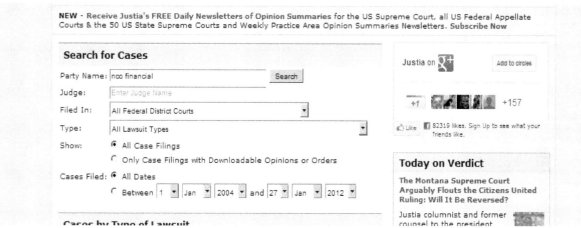

Click the **search** button. All of the cases will com e up. Now click on the state you live in. 29 court cases come up. Look for ones with FDCPA violations in them.

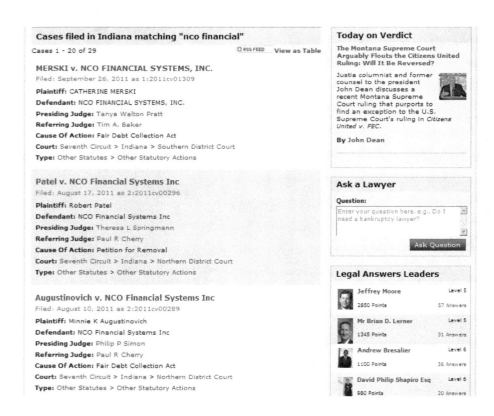

Cases by State

Alabama	Louisiana	Oklahoma
Alaska	Maine	Oregon
Arizona	Maryland	Pennsylvania
Arkansas	Massachusetts	Rhode Island
California	Michigan	South Carolina
Colorado	Minnesota	South Dakota
Connecticut	Mississippi	Tennessee
Delaware	Missouri	Texas
District of Columbia	Montana	Utah
Florida	Nebraska	Vermont
Georgia	Nevada	Virginia
Hawaii	New Hampshire	Washington
Idaho	New Jersey	West Virginia
Illinois	New Mexico	Wisconsin
Indiana	New York	Wyoming
Iowa	North Carolina	Guam
Kansas	North Dakota	Mariana Islands
Kentucky	Ohio	Puerto Rico

Cases filed in Indiana matching "nco financial"

Cases 1 - 20 of 29   RSS FEED   View as Table

MERSKI v. NCO FINANCIAL SYSTEMS, INC.
Filed: September 26, 2011 as 1:2011cv01309
Plaintiff: CATHERINE MERSKI
Defendant: NCO FINANCIAL SYSTEMS, INC.
Presiding Judge: Tanya Walton Pratt
Referring Judge: Tim A. Baker
Cause Of Action: Fair Debt Collection Act
Court: Seventh Circuit > Indiana > Southern District Court
Type: Other Statutes > Other Statutory Actions

Patel v. NCO Financial Systems Inc
Filed: August 17, 2011 as 2:2011cv00296
Plaintiff: Robert Patel
Defendant: NCO Financial Systems Inc
Presiding Judge: Theresa L Springmann
Referring Judge: Paul R Cherry
Cause Of Action: Petition for Removal
Court: Seventh Circuit > Indiana > Northern District Court
Type: Other Statutes > Other Statutory Actions

Augustinovich v. NCO Financial Systems Inc
Filed: August 10, 2011 as 2:2011cv00289
Plaintiff: Minnie K Augustinovich
Defendant: NCO Financial Systems Inc
Presiding Judge: Philip P Simon
Referring Judge: Paul R Cherry
Cause Of Action: Fair Debt Collection Act
Court: Seventh Circuit > Indiana > Northern District Court
Type: Other Statutes > Other Statutory Actions

Today on Verdict

The Montana Supreme Court Arguably Flouts the Citizens United Ruling: Will It Be Reversed?

Justia columnist and former counsel to the president John Dean discusses a recent Montana Supreme Court ruling that purports to find an exception to the U.S. Supreme Court's ruling in *Citizens United v. FEC.*

By John Dean

Ask a Lawyer

Question:

Enter your question here. e.g., Do I need a bankruptcy lawyer?

Ask Question

Legal Answers Leaders

Jeffrey Moore		Level 5
2850 Points		57 Answers
Mr Brian D. Lerner		Level 5
1345 Points		31 Answers
Andrew Bresalier		Level 6
1100 Points		36 Answers
David Philip Shapiro Esq		Level 6
980 Points		20 Answers

Let's go to the Pacer website to find more info on this case. Click on the **find a case** link. Register with those site if you haven't done so yet. Do a party name search for NCO Financial Systems in your state.

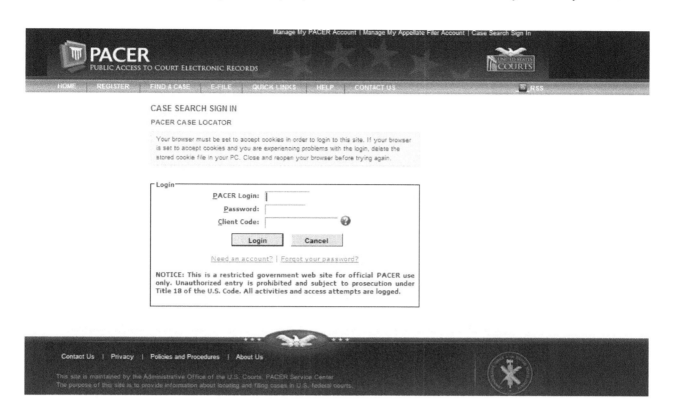

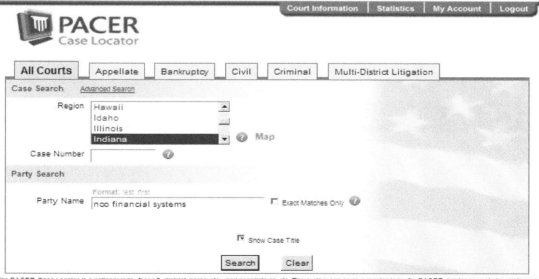

If you look on the second page of search results you will see the same case that was listed on Justia.

| ✕ Find: | merski | | | | Previous | Next | ✐ | Options ▾ | 1 match |

~~NCO FINANCIAL SYSTEMS, INC. (dft) insdce~~ ~~1:2007-cv-00101~~ WOODS v. NATIONAL FINANCIAL SYSTEMS, INC. et al	890	03/12/2007	05/16/2008
72 NCO FINANCIAL SYSTEMS, INC. (dft) insdce 1:2004-cv-00502 BURROUGHS v. NCO FINANCIAL SYSTEMS, INC.	890	03/15/2004	05/24/2004
73 NCO FINANCIAL SYSTEMS, INC. (dft) insdce 1:2005-cv-00180 ALSMAN et al v. NCO FINANCIAL SYSTEMS, INC.	890	02/04/2005	03/10/2005
74 NCO FINANCIAL SYSTEMS, INC. (dft) insdce 3:2005-cv-00077 KOPSHEVER et al v. INDIANA 8, LLC et al	480	04/13/2005	06/28/2005
75 NCO FINANCIAL SYSTEMS, INC. (dft) insdce 1:2005-cv-01512 EILER v. NCO FINANCIAL SYSTEMS, INC.	890	10/12/2005	01/13/2006
76 NCO FINANCIAL SYSTEMS, INC. (dft) insdce 1:2005-cv-01541 MCCORMICK v. NCO FINANCIAL SYSTEMS, INC.	890	10/14/2005	01/13/2006
77 NCO FINANCIAL SYSTEMS, INC. (dft) insdce 1:2005-cv-01674 PATTERSON et al v. NCO FINANCIAL SYSTEMS, INC.	890	11/09/2005	01/30/2006
78 NCO FINANCIAL SYSTEMS, INC. (dft) insdce 1:2006-cv-00076 GEORGE v. NCO FINANCIAL SYSTEMS, INC.	890	01/18/2006	03/27/2006
79 NCO FINANCIAL SYSTEMS, INC. (dft) insdce 1:2006-cv-00470 SIMS et al v. NCO FINANCIAL SYSTEMS, INC.	890	03/22/2006	08/22/2006
80 NCO FINANCIAL SYSTEMS, INC. (dft) insdce 1:2007-cv-01183 KENOYER v. WYSE FINANCIAL SERVICES, INC. et al	890	09/17/2007	12/04/2007
81 NCO FINANCIAL SYSTEMS, INC. (dft) insdce 1:2008-cv-00325 RANKIN v. NCO FINANCIAL SYSTEMS, INC.	890	03/12/2008	04/16/2008
82 NCO FINANCIAL SYSTEMS, INC. (dft) insdce 1:2008-cv-01615 MINTUN et al v. BLITT and GAINES, P.C. et al	890	12/01/2008	03/10/2009
83 NCO FINANCIAL SYSTEMS, INC. (dft) insdce 1:2010-cv-00296 WIRE v. NCO FINANCIAL SYSTEMS, INC.	480	03/11/2010	06/22/2010
84 NCO FINANCIAL SYSTEMS, INC. (dft) insdce 1:2011-cv-00256 HARRIS v. NCO FINANACIAL SYSTEMS, INC.	480	02/18/2011	04/19/2011
85 NCO FINANCIAL SYSTEMS, INC. (dft) insdce 1:2011-cv-00315 MAYER v. NCO FINANCIAL SYSTEMS, INC.	890	03/02/2011	11/15/2011
86 NCO FINANCIAL SYSTEMS, INC. (dft) insdce 1:2011-cv-00994 MCHALE v. NCO FINANCIAL SYSTEMS, INC. et al	890	07/26/2011	10/24/2011
87 NCO FINANCIAL SYSTEMS, INC. (dft) insdce 1:2011-cv-01025 RAMIREZ v. NCO FINANCIAL SYSTEMS, INC.	480	07/29/2011	11/16/2011
88 NCO FINANCIAL SYSTEMS, INC. (dft) insdce 1:2011-cv-01309 MERSKI v. NCO FINANCIAL SYSTEMS, INC.	890	09/26/2011	11/16/2011

Previous 1 **2** Next

CM/ECF   Query   Reports ▾   Utilities ▾   Logout

Query

Alias
Associated Cases
Attorney
Docket Report ...
Filers
History/Documents...
Party
Related Transactions...
View a Document

Now click on the **case history** and you can see what happened in the case. Looks like both sides made a deal. You can also find the law firm that represented the Plaintiff who brought the suit against NCO for violating the FDCPA. Click on number 1 to see what the case is about. Remember it will cost a few pennies every time you view a page.

Tim A. Baker, referral
Date filed: 09/26/2011
Date terminated: 11/16/2011
Date of last update: 11/16/2011

History

Doc. No.	Dates		Description
1	Filed:	09/26/2011	Complaint
	Entered:	09/27/2011	
2	Filed:	09/26/2011	Civil Cover Sheet
	Entered:	09/27/2011	
3	Filed:	09/26/2011	Receipt
	Entered:	09/27/2011	
4	Filed:	09/26/2011	Summons Issued
	Entered:	09/27/2011	
5	Filed:	09/26/2011	Notice of Appearance
	Entered:	09/27/2011	
6	Filed:	09/26/2011	Notice of Appearance
	Entered:	09/27/2011	
7	Filed:	09/26/2011	Notice of Appearance
	Entered:	09/27/2011	
8	Filed:	09/26/2011	Magistrate Judge's Notice of Availability to Exercise Jurisdiction
	Entered:	09/27/2011	
9	Filed & Entered:	10/04/2011	Return of Service
10	Filed & Entered:	10/17/2011	Order
11	Filed & Entered:	11/14/2011	Notice of Voluntary Dismissal
12	Filed & Entered:	11/16/2011	Closed Dismissed

ECF   Query   Reports ▾   Utilities ▾   Logout

Document Selection Menu

Select the document you wish to view.

Document Number: 1   5 pages   152 kb

Attachment	Description		
1	Exhibit Group A- Information re NCO Financial	4 pages	122 kb
2	US Bankruptcy Court petition	4 pages	231 kb
3	Exhibit C-Notice of Chapter 7 Bankruptcy Case, Meeting of Creditors and Deadlin	3 pages	190 kb

View All or Download All   16 pages   0.7 mb

If you are going to be representing yourself in court, be sure to look at the civil cases that the collection agencies are involved in. This will give you a good idea of what FDCPA violations they get sued for. You can find a wealth of information on Justia and Pacer. Below is the complaint against NCO Financial.

IN THE UNITED STATES DISTRICT COURT
FOR THE SOUTHERN DISTRICT OF INDIANA
INDIANAPOLIS DIVISION

FILED
U.S. DISTRICT COURT
INDIANAPOLIS DIVISION
2011 SEP 26 PM 4:42
SOUTHERN DISTRICT
OF INDIANA
LAURA A. BRIGGS
CLERK

Catherine Merski,	)	
Plaintiff,	)	
	)	
v.	)	No.
	)	
NCO Financial Systems, Inc. a	)	**1:11 -cv- 1309 TWP -TAB**
Pennsylvania corporation,	)	
Defendant.	)	Jury Demanded

COMPLAINT

Plaintiff, Catherine Merski, brings this action under the Fair Debt Collection Practices Act, 15 U.S.C. § 1692, et seq. ("FDCPA"), for a finding that Defendant's debt collection actions violate the FDCPA, and to recover damages for Defendant's violation of the FDCPA, and alleges:

JURISDICTION AND VENUE

1.   This Court has jurisdiction pursuant to § 1692k(d) of the FDCPA, and 28 U.S.C. § 1331.

2.   Venue is proper in this District because: a) the acts and transactions occurred here; b) Plaintiff resides here; and, c) Defendant resides and transacts business here.

PARTIES

3.   Plaintiff, Catherine Merski ("Merski"), is a citizen of the State of Indiana, residing in the Southern District of Indiana, from whom Defendant attempted to collect a delinquent consumer debt allegedly owed for electric service.

4.   Defendant, NCO Financial Systems, Inc. ("NCO"), is a Pennsylvania

On page 12 you can find out who the attorney is that represented the consumer. Now you have all of the information for your second validation letter: case name, case number, and the law firm that represents the client suing the collection agency.

Case 11-09787-JKC-7   Filed 08/02/11   EOD 08/02/11 ...35:24   Pg 3 of 35

B1 (Official Form 1)(4/10)   Page 3

Voluntary Petition	Name of Debtor(s):
(This page must be completed and filed in every case)	Merski, Catherine Lynn

Signatures

Signature(s) of Debtor(s) (Individual/Joint)

I declare under penalty of perjury that the information provided in this petition is true and correct.
[If petitioner is an individual whose debts are primarily consumer debts and has chosen to file under chapter 7] I am aware that I may proceed under chapter 7, 11, 12, or 13 of title 11, United States Code, understand the relief available under each such chapter, and choose to proceed under chapter 7.
[If no attorney represents me and no bankruptcy petition preparer signs the petition] I have obtained and read the notice required by 11 U.S.C. §343(b).

I request relief in accordance with the chapter of title 11, United States Code, specified in this petition.

X /s/ Catherine Lynn Merski
Signature of Debtor Catherine Lynn Merski

X _____
Signature of Joint Debtor

_____
Telephone Number (If not represented by attorney)

August 2, 2011
Date

Signature of Attorney*

X /s/ Steven J. Halbert
Signature of Attorney for Debtor(s)

Steven J. Halbert 14254-02
Printed Name of Attorney for Debtor(s)

Steven J. Halbert
Firm Name

11805 N. Pennsylvania St.
Carmel, IN 46032

_____
Address

Email: SHalbertLaw@aol.com
(317) 706-6762 Fax: (317) 706-6763
Telephone Number

August 2, 2011
Date

*In a case in which § 707(b)(4)(D) applies, this signature also constitutes a certification that the attorney has no knowledge after an inquiry that the information in the schedules is incorrect.

Signature of Debtor (Corporation/Partnership)

I declare under penalty of perjury that the information provided in this petition is true and correct, and that I have been authorized to file this petition on behalf of the debtor.

The debtor requests relief in accordance with the chapter of title 11, United States Code, specified in this petition.

X _____
Signature of Authorized Individual

_____
Printed Name of Authorized Individual

_____
Title of Authorized Individual

_____
Date

Signature of a Foreign Representative

I declare under penalty of perjury that the information provided in this petition is true and correct, that I am the foreign representative of a debtor in a foreign proceeding, and that I am authorized to file this petition.

(Check only one box.)

☐ I request relief in accordance with chapter 15 of title 11, United States Code. Certified copies of the documents required by 11 U.S.C. §1515 are attached.

☐ Pursuant to 11 U.S.C. §1511, I request relief in accordance with the chapter of title 11 specified in this petition. A certified copy of the order granting recognition of the foreign main proceeding is attached.

X _____
Signature of Foreign Representative

_____
Printed Name of Foreign Representative

_____
Date

Signature of Non-Attorney Bankruptcy Petition Preparer

I declare under penalty of perjury that (1) I am a bankruptcy petition preparer as defined in 11 U.S.C. § 110; (2) I prepared this document for compensation and have provided the debtor with a copy of this document and the notices and information required under 11 U.S.C. §§ 110(b), 110(h), and 342(b); and, (3) if rules or guidelines have been promulgated pursuant to 11 U.S.C. § 110(h) setting a maximum fee for services chargeable by bankruptcy petition preparers, I have given the debtor notice of the maximum amount before preparing any document for filing for a debtor or accepting any fee from the debtor, as required in that section. Official Form 19 is attached.

_____
Printed Name and title, if any, of Bankruptcy Petition Preparer

_____
Social-Security number (If the bankruptcy petition preparer is not an individual, state the Social-Security number of the officer, principal, responsible person or partner of the bankruptcy petition preparer.)(Required by 11 U.S.C. § 110.)

_____
Address

X _____

_____
Date

Signature of Bankruptcy Petition Preparer or officer, principal, responsible person, or partner whose Social-Security number is provided above.

Names and Social-Security numbers of all other individuals who prepared or assisted in preparing this document unless the bankruptcy petition preparer is not an individual:

If more than one person prepared this document, attach additional sheets conforming to the appropriate official form for each person.

A bankruptcy petition preparer's failure to comply with the provisions of title 11 and the Federal Rules of Bankruptcy Procedure may result in fines or imprisonment or both 11 U.S.C. §110; 18 U.S.C. §156.

Here is a notice that the collector has given up. Bye bye! This process can go on for years, and the longer it goes on, the less the debt is worth. So in the future you can take an offer of a couple cents on the dollar from a junk debt buyer that purchased your debt. Or you can wait until the statue of limitations has run out. Just remember, everything has to be in writing and recorded when making deals with collection agencies or junk debt buyers. Only pay them with a money order from the post office or grocery store. Never give them your bank information! Never trust them!

NCO Financial Systems, Inc.
507 Prudential Road
Horsham, PA 19044
1-866-305-9426

Office Hours: 8:00 a.m. - 9:00 p.m. Monday through Thursday,
8:00 a.m. - 5:00 p.m. Friday, 8:00 a.m. - 12:00 noon Saturday

May 03, 2011

███████████████

Re: Our Reference No(s).   Creditor(s)
████████████   Capital One Bank (USA), N.A. ████████████

Dear ██████████:

Thank you for your inquiry regarding the above-referenced account. This letter is pursuant to your specific request for a response. Please be advised that the above-referenced account has been placed in a status to prevent further collection activity by NCO. Further inquiry regarding the underlying debt may be directed to Capital One Bank (USA), N.A., 2100 Maywill Street, Richmond, VA 23230.

We appreciate the opportunity to respond to your inquiry.

Very truly yours,

Sharon A. Wander
Consumer Affairs Production Manager

This is an attempt to collect a debt. Any information obtained will be used for that purpose. This is a communication from a debt collector.

Calls to or from NCO Financial Systems, Inc. may be monitored or recorded for quality assurance.

Here is another example from NCO.

⟡·NCO

NCO Financial Systems, Inc.
507 Prudential Road | Horsham, PA 19044
Toll Free: 800.550.9619 | Fax: 866.269.8669
Hours of Operation: M-F 8:00am-5:00pm ET

January 11, 2012

███████
███████

Re: Our Reference No(s). Creditor(s)
    ███████   Citibank, N.A.
                   Account No.: ███████

Dear ███████

Thank you for your inquiry regarding the above-referenced account. Please be advised that the above-referenced account is closed in our office.

According to our files, we have not reported the above-referenced account to a credit bureau. Please be advised that NCO Financial Systems, Inc. cannot effect a change to how any other company or entity may have listed the account on your credit profile.

We appreciate the opportunity to respond to your inquiry.

Very truly yours,

Jamal Hutchinson
Consumer Affairs Representative II

This is an attempt to collect a debt. Any information obtained will be used for that purpose. This is a communication from a debt collector.

Calls to or from NCO Financial Systems, Inc. may be monitored or recorded for quality assurance.

TRICKS THAT THE COLLECTION AGENCIES USE

We have talked about some of the dirty tricks the collection agencies use, but have only skimmed on the surface. There are literally over 100 different tactics that these bottom feeders will use to get at your money. And some of the worst ones are inconceivable, like setting up a fake court with fake sheriffs. It sounds unbelievable, but it happened. You can read about it here: http://www.ronpaulforums.com/showthread.php?266143-New-scam-Collection-Agency-has-fake-courts-and-sheriffs

It's important to understand that there is nothing beneath these companies. They will try anything. So you need to be aware of some of the common tricks the collection agencies will use. But before we go over that, let's review the Federal Debt Collection Practices Act. You can view it in its entirety here: http://www.ftc.gov/bcp/edu/pubs/consumer/credit/cre27.pdf

Let's summarize this act. Under the FDCPA, collection agencies are basically not allowed to lie, harass you, curse at you, or threaten you. Note: harassment is anything you deem to be harassing. Collection agencies can't call before 8am or after 9pm, or charge more than you actually owe, unless your contract with the original creditor allows them to do so. And if you request validation of the debt, or proof, they must prove you owe them money or give up all collection efforts. Those are some of the main points that you probably already know about. Now let's go over some of the other tricks that some collectors like to use.

1. Claim they already sent you a collection letter. This has happened to me. The collector calls up and requests money. They claim they sent the letter and I must have threw it away by mistake. This collector was trying to prevent me from requesting validation in the 30 days that the FDCPA allows. They wouldn't even give me their address. I had to look it up online quickly and send out the request. If you get a phone call from a collector, always get the company name and write it down.

2. Send the collection letter to the wrong address. Sometimes debt collectors will send the collection letter to a previous address. You won't get it and they will then take you to court without you even knowing. Since there was no request to validate the debt and you didn't show up to court, the judge will rule in favor of the collector.

3. Claim they can validate the debt over the phone. This is a lie. A collector cannot validate anything over the phone. And would you believe anything he or she said? Of course not.

4. Call your neighbors or relatives. This is a way to humiliate you into paying. They will even call up your employer if they know where you work. If you want all communication to be through the mail only, write a cease and desist letter to the collector. Just say that collection agency X, under the Fair Debt Collection Practices Act, must cease and desist all attempts to collect the alleged debt, except for written communication sent through the United States Postal Service, Fedex, or UPS.

5. Tell you your debt is too big or too small for a settlement. This tactic usually comes from the original creditor. It's just plain wrong. Even a $25 debt can be settled. The smaller the debt, the less likely you are going to end up in court.

6. Threaten to take you to court. It is illegal for a collector to threaten to sue you if they have no plans on doing so. Instead of saying they will sue you, they usually say, "if you are not going to pay, then we will have to take the next step!" If that is the case, try to get them to threaten a lawsuit. Even ask them if they will sue you. Then find out the bar license number of a lawyer that works there, if there is one. Often, the agency is owned by 1 or 2 disbarred lawyers. Next, file complaints with the Attorney General,

Federal Trade Commission, and Better Business Bureau.

7. Send you deceptive collection letters. Some collection agencies will use the logo of their client on the collection letter in order to make you think you are still dealing with the original creditor, and you don't need to validate the debt. Or they will try to make their company sound like a law firm. Google the name of the company and see what the blogs are saying. Don't be surprised to find out that the lawyer that owns the company has been disbarred or arrested.

8. After you pay the collection agency, they sell your account to another collector. If you make deals with the devil, you will eventually get burned. If you pay collection agencies over the phone without any legal proof, some of them will take your money and run.

9. Agree to pay a small amount, and then get your account cleaned out. Some collection agencies have been known to make great deals if you can pay over the phone with a check. Once they get the number, they change the numbers and clean out your account. Never pay a collection agency over the phone. Never give them any financial details, like your bank name. Never make deals will a collector that does not own your debt. And always get everything in writing, and recorded over the phone when making deals with the owner of your debt.

10. Try to collect someone else's debt. I think we have all gotten phone calls from collectors looking for someone you have never heard of. Often, those mistakes are the result of skip tracing software. If they keep harassing you, then send a cease and desist letter to the debt collector. This will work for collection agencies, but not for the original creditor.

11. Try to lower your credit score to force you to call them. If they can ruin your credit rating with hard pulls, then they will ruin your chances of buying a home or car. Even if the debt is disputed with the credit rating agencies, be sure to check your credit report periodically.

12. Change the age the debt. Collectors will often try to extend the statute of limitations, giving them more time to collect on a debt. To do this, they must change the date of the debt. It doesn't matter what they say, the actual timing for the Statute of Limitations starts when you made your last payment, or your last payment plus 30 days. This is when you actually defaulted, and a cause of action for breach of contract has occurred. This is why many collectors ask for a small payment of $10 to put the debt on hold. By agreeing to pay on the debt, collectors can use the payment as evidence in court that you are not disputing the debt. This will allow the statute of limitations to start all over again.

13. Lie about the date the letter was sent. Check the date on the collection letter you received, and the actual date you received it. Sometimes collectors will change the dates, leaving you with less time to request validation for the debt.

14. File a lawsuit without sending a collection letter. Some of the scumbags in the collection industry will actually sue you without sending you any requests for payment. Without seeing the collection letter, many people will not know that they could have validated the debt and stopped the collection efforts.

15. Adding on fees or interest. Only the original signed contract can stipulate whether or not a collection agency or junk debt buyer can tack on any fees for their collection efforts. You need to see the original contract before a collection agency can attempt to increase your debt.

15. Send a fake Affidavit of Debt. After you request validation, you may receive a fraudulent letter from someone at the collection agency claiming to be an expert that has now validated your debt. Don't buy it.

16. Refusing to properly disclose their identity. By law, a collection agency must provide you with an accurate representation. That means they have to disclose their company name, address, and phone number. The caller must also give you his name or company ID number if asked. You need to be on the watch for callers claiming they are from the collection agency "legal department". In many cases, a legal department doesn't exist. If they make this claim, ask to speak to one of their lawyers and ask for their bar card number and which state they got it from, which you can then use to look up the lawyer online. Many state websites also post disciplinary actions and disbarment history for its lawyers.

17. Sign your name for you. Whenever you sign your name on a validation request or correspondence, sign it differently than you normally would. Use your initials whenever dealing with collection agencies. That way if you see your initials on a "copy" of the original contract, you will know it's a fake.

18. Get you not to show up to court. This is a real dirty tactic that some collectors will use if they think you are afraid to go to court. Here is how it works. They will send you a summons to go to court. Then call you and make an incredible offer. If you agree to the deal, they will cancel the court case and tell you not to go to court. The only problem is, they never cancel the case and win the full amount because you didn't show up to court. If you get a summons, show up to court if the case ends up there. Most debt cases end before the actual bench trial. Often, the collector in court only has your name, social security number, amount owed, and nothing else. That is hardly proof of anything. If the collection agency sues 100 people at a time, 90% of the cases will be default judgements because the consumers didn't show up, or didn't answer the summons.

18. Violating the Telephone Consumer Protection Act. If you received a pre-recorded message on your cell phone telling you to "hold for the next available representative" or "press 1 if your name is this", then you might be able to file a complaint with the Federal Communications Commission, Attorney General, and Better Business Bureau. And just like the FDCPA, you can sue in your local court for every violation that the collector committed. Here is what needs to happen for a TCPA violation to occur. The collection company needs to call you on a phone number that you did not give to the original creditor. And if they don't have permission to call you on a specific phone line, then they cannot use an auto-dialer to call you. If you contact the original creditor and revoke permission to call you, and request all communication in writing, then you can often catch collection agencies violating the TCPA when they call on a number without permission for auto-dialling.

19. Offering you a settlement. Never admit to owing a debt over the phone. This tactic is an easy way to get a person to admit that they owe the debt while the phone call is being recorded. They can use this recording in court if needed. If you are going to get a deal, it should come from the original creditor that owns the debt. If you think the original creditor is ready for a settlement, call them up and ask them about a settlement for your alleged debt.

20. Not disclosing that they are trying to collect a debt. Sometimes collectors will throw in this phrase ("this call is an attempt to collect a debt") at the end of the call, instead of the beginning. If you are recording the call, and they are asking for a payment without disclosing they are trying to collect a debt, simply hang up on them and send a copy of the tape to the attorney general. You might also want to ask a debt collection lawyer if you have a good case for litigation. You could sue them for $1000 for this violation.

21. Pulling your credit report. Hard pulls on your credit report actually lower your credit score and are only allowed when you give permission to do so, like when you need credit to buy a car. Collection companies do hard pulls to see if you are worth suing or not. This could be a violation of the Fair Credit Reporting Act 15 U.S.C. 1681q (FCRA). Unfortunately, the case law just doesn't exist yet to support a blatant violation of the FCRA. It really depends on whether a collection agency has "permissible purpose" or not, and if the collection agency is "involved in the credit transaction" in some way. If you ask 50 people their opinion on this issue, you will get 25 people that say the collector broke the law, and 25 that say the collector did nothing wrong. Both sides, however, do agree that it hurts your credit score. We will talk more about this later on in the book.

FILING COMPLAINTS

If you have been the victim of a violation of the FDCPA, then you need to file a claim with the Federal Trade Commission, the state Attorney General they do business in, and the Better Business Bureau in the state they reside in. By throwing the first punch, this will send a strong message that you are ready to fight them head on.

Below you will see a debt collection letter from Global Credit & Collection Corp. Not only does this letter claim that the debtor might be sued, but the debtor might also be charged addition fees which are not able to be charged without proof of contract. To the least sophisticated consumer, this appears to be quite confusing. In my eyes, it appears to be a violation of the FDCPA. If you think it may be a violation, file complaints immediately.

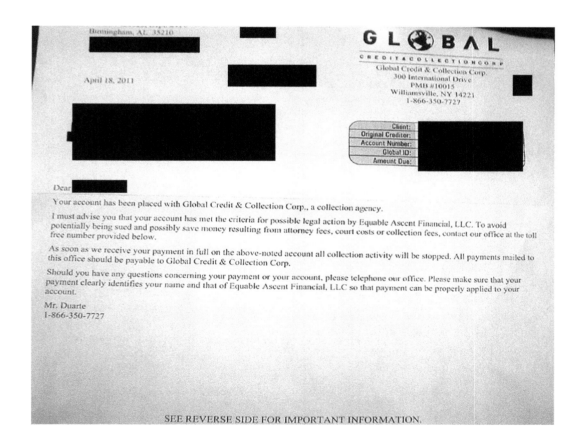

Step 1. Go the Federal Trade Commission's website and file a complaint online. It's quick and easy.
https://www.ftccomplaintassistant.gov/FTC_Wizard.aspx?Lang=en

Step 2. File a complaint with the Attorney General in the state that the collector does business in. Global Credit & Collections has an office in New York, so the debtor filed a claim with New York Attorney General Eric T. Schneiderman. Just print out the forms online, and mail them in.

ATTORNEY GENERAL ERIC T. SCHNEIDERMAN
STATE OF NEW YORK
OFFICE OF THE ATTORNEY GENERAL
BUREAU OF CONSUMER FRAUDS AND PROTECTION
350 Main Street - Main Place Tower, Suite 300A
Buffalo, NY 14202-0341
Tel. (716) 853-8404   Fax (716) 853-8414

COMPLAINT FORM
Consumer Hotline   For Hearing Impaired
1 (800) 771-7755   TDD 1 (800) 788-9898
http://www.ag.ny.gov

1. PLEASE BE SURE TO COMPLAIN TO THE COMPANY OR INDIVIDUAL *BEFORE* FILING.
2. PLEASE *TYPE* OR PRINT CLEARLY IN DARK INK.
3. YOU MUST COMPLETE THE *ENTIRE* FORM. INCOMPLETE OR UNCLEAR FORMS WILL BE RETURNED TO YOU.
4. MAKE SURE YOU ENCLOSE *COPIES* OF IMPORTANT PAPERS CONCERNING YOUR TRANSACTION.

CONSUMER

YOUR NAME	HOME TELEPHONE NUMBER
STREET ADDRESS	BUSINESS TELEPHONE NUMBER
CITY/TOWN	COUNTY STATE ZIP

COMPLAINT

NAME OF SELLER OR PROVIDER OF SERVICES	NAME OF OTHER SELLER OR PROVIDER OF SERVICES
GLOBAL CREDIT & COLLECTION CORP.	
STREET ADDRESS 300 INTERNATIONAL DR. PMB 10015	STREET ADDRESS
CITY/TOWN WILLIAMSVILLE STATE NY ZIP 14221	CITY/TOWN STATE ZIP
TELEPHONE NUMBER 866-350-7727	TELEPHONE NUMBER

DATE OF TRANSACTION	COST OF PRODUCT OR SERVICE $	HOW PAID (Check those which apply) ☐ Cash ☐ Check ☐ Credit Card ☐ Other

DID YOU SIGN A CONTRACT? ☐ Yes ☐ No	WHERE DID YOU SIGN THE CONTRACT?	DATE SIGNED

WAS PRODUCT OR SERVICE ADVERTISED? ☐ Yes ☐ No	WHERE WAS IT ADVERTISED?	DATE ADVERTISED

TYPE OF COMPLAINT (e.g. car, mail order, etc. Use the reverse side of this form to provide details)
VIOLATION OF FDCPA

DATE YOU COMPLAINED TO THE COMPANY OR INDIVIDUAL 4/25/11 ☑ By Mail ☐ By Telephone ☐ In Person	PERSON CONTACTED	JOB TITLE

NATURE OF RESPONSE	DATE OF RESPONSE

HAS MATTER BEEN SUBMITTED TO ANOTHER AGENCY OR ATTORNEY? (If "Yes," give name and address)
☑ Yes ☐ No   FEDERAL TRADE COMMISION (FTC COMPLAINTASSISTANT.GOV)

IS COURT ACTION PENDING? (Please describe as necessary)
☐ Yes ☑ No

ADDITIONAL INFORMATION

MANUFACTURER OF PRODUCT	PRODUCT MODEL OR SERIAL NUMBER
ADDRESS	WARRANTY EXPIRATION DATE

DID BUSINESS ARRANGE FINANCING? (If "Yes," give name and address of bank or finance company)
☐ Yes ☐ No

PLEASE DESCRIBE COMPLAINT ON REVERSE SIDE

CFABFR (01/11)

BRIEFLY DESCRIBE YOUR COMPLAINT: GLOBAL CREDIT & COLLECTION CORP.
SENT ME A COLLECTION LETTER THREATENING TO
POSSIBLY SUE ME AND CHARGE ME ~~ATTORNEY FEES~~
ATTORNEY FEES, COURT COSTS, AND COLLECTION FEES. GLOBAL
DOES NOT OWN THE DEBT AND THEIR CLIENT, EQUABLE
ASCENT FINANCIAL, LLC CANNOT CHARGE ME ANY
COLLECTION FEES OR MAKE THREATS. ████████
████████████████████████████. ALSO
THIS IS THE ONLY NOTICE I HAVE RECEIVED. MY ACCOUNT
HAS NOT MET ANY CRITERIA FOR LEGAL ACTION.

WHAT FORM OF RELIEF ARE YOU SEEKING? (e.g., exchange, repair or money back, etc.) I WOULD LIKE
THE STATE OF NEW YORK TO FINE GLOBAL CREDIT & COLLETION CORP.

WHO REFERRED YOU TO THIS OFFICE? FAIR-DEBT-COLLECTION.COM

READ THE FOLLOWING BEFORE SIGNING BELOW

PLEASE ATTACH TO THIS FORM **PHOTOCOPIES** of any papers involved (contracts, warranties, bills received, canceled checks, correspondence, etc.). **DO NOT SEND ORIGINALS.**

NOTE: In order to resolve your complaint, we may send a copy of this form to the person or firm about whom you are complaining.

In filing this complaint, I understand that the Attorney General is not my private attorney, but represents the public in enforcing laws designed to protect the public from misleading or unlawful business practices. I also understand that if I have any questions concerning my legal rights or responsibilities, I should contact a private attorney. I have no objection to the contents of this complaint being forwarded to the business or person the complaint is directed against. The above complaint is true and accurate to the best of my knowledge.

I also understand that any false statements made in this complaint are punishable as a Class A Misdemeanor under Section 175.30 and/or Section 210.45 of the Penal Law.

Signature: _____████████_____   Date: ___████_____

HAVE YOU ENCLOSED COPIES OF IMPORTANT PAPERS?

Return to: Office of the Attorney General
               Bureau of Consumer Frauds and Protection
               Buffalo Regional Office
               Main Place Tower, Suite 300A
               350 Main Street
               Buffalo, NY 14202

Step 3. File a complaint with the Better Business Bureau. To do this, go to bbb.org and type in the city and state of the collection agency. In my case, it was Williamsville, NY. That took me to the proper BBB website, http://upstateny.bbb.org.

Find the **file a complaint** link.

Begin the process by answering a few questions.

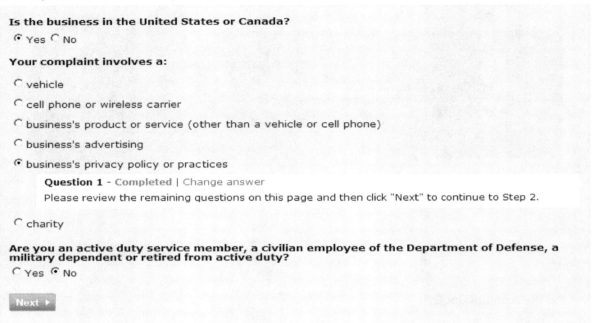

Next type in the business name.

Once you have located the business, the site will redirect you to Ontario, Canada's complaint system. It appears that this company is not primarily located in the USA. Follow the instructions from here on out and type in your complaint.

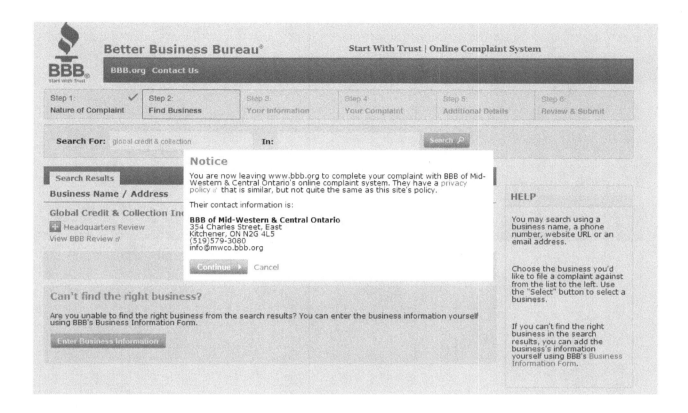

On the BBB site you can also find out some information about their recent complaints and how many of them are open.

Reason for Rating

BBB rating is based on 16 factors. Get the details about the factors considered.

Factors that *lowered* Global Credit & Collection Inc.'s rating include:

> › 27 complaints filed against business that were not resolved.

Factors that *raised* Global Credit & Collection Inc.'s rating include:

> › Length of time business has been operating.
> › Complaint volume filed with BBB for business of this size.
> › Response to 122 complaint(s) filed against business.
> › BBB has sufficient background information on this business.

Customer Complaints Summary

122 complaints closed with BBB in last 3 years	111 closed in last 12 months	
Complaint Type	**Total Closed Complaints**
Advertising / Sales Issues	1
Billing / Collection Issues	98
Problems with Product / Service	23
Delivery Issues	0
Guarantee / Warranty Issues	0
Total Closed Complaints	122

Complaint Details | Definitions | BBB Complaint Process | File a Complaint

Step 4. You can also file a complaint with the original creditor, or whoever legally owns the debt. Find out where to mail complaints to and then send a letter letting the original creditor know that their client, the collection agency, is violating the FDCPA, and you are considering taking legal action against them. Don't go into detail. Just let them know that their client is breaking the law. Nobody wants to get complaints sent to their boss, not even bill collectors.

STEP 4 – GOING TO COURT

The opinions contained in this book are NOT legal advice, and should NOT be interpreted as legal advice, or council. Always consult the services of an attorney whenever you need legal advice.

If you do end up getting sued by a credit card company or collection agency, the best advice is to get a lawyer fast. They have experience dealing with bill collectors and can often win cases quickly. If you are able to save up some money, you might want to check out www.legalmatch.com or http://www.naca.net or http://www.budhibbs.com for a qualified debt collection attorney in your area. Bud Hibbs also list some of the worst collection agencies in the business on his website. It is definitely worth a read. Another idea might be to find a debt collection/bankruptcy attorney in your area who charges a flat fee for representation and a bench trial. Some attorneys will do this for $500 hundred dollars or more. That's a great deal considering many attorneys charge several hundred dollars per hour for representation. You can also post your legal questions for free at www.avvo.com. Lawyers will answer your questions in hopes of attracting new business.

If you are broke, then you will be forced to represent yourself in court, or make a deal with the original creditor. "Pro Se," or representing yourself in court, is a growing trend in America. It's much cheaper to represent yourself, and often just as effective as long as the case is simple. So let's go over the basic legal strategies for you and the bill collector suing you.

First off, the collection agency or original creditor suing you is going to try to get a summary judgment against you. They don't want a long and expensive trial with many depositions, especially if you only owe a few thousand dollars or less. The bill collectors are essentially using the same tactic that you will use. Win the case with either a motion to dismiss or a motion for summary judgment before anyone has to go before the judge. Everyone wants to keep the case on paper, it's much cheaper that way. Specifically, your game plan will involve attacking the credibility and legal standing that the plaintiff has. You will do this by fighting the plaintiff's affidavit of debt with a motion to strike, attacking their right to attorney fees, attacking the assignment of debt, and compelling the plaintiff to answer your discovery requests. If you can get the court to agree to any of these, the plaintiff might try to make a deal, or just drop the case before it gets too expensive. You see, the collection agencies are not used to fighting since most of the time the debtor simply doesn't show up to court, and the judge usually grants a quick default judgment.

If the original creditor or collection agency wins a judgment, there are three main ways that they can legally take your money: **bank levy** (non-wage garnishment), **wage garnishment**, or **lien** on your home or property. Here is the breakdown. If you have some money in your bank account, the collector will try to get a judgment against you allowing them to clean out your account, leaving you with $0. If you have a decent job, the collector will try to get a judgment allowing them to collect a percentage of your income. And if you own a home, the collector will try to get a judgment for a lien on your property. This means that once the property is sold, they will take their cut. Or they can tell a sheriff to serve a Writ of Execution, allowing them to seize any property you own, like your car, to be auctioned off.

There are a few tactics you can use to become more judgment proof, meaning that even if they beat you in court they still will win nothing. It makes no sense to sue a person who appears judgment proof. You can't take something from someone that doesn't exist. If you earn $150 a week, don't own a house, and don't own an expensive car, then you are pretty much judgment proof since a court is not going to order you to pay anything at this time. If you are judgment proof and a collection company wins a judgment against you, they could force you back to court to check on your financial status over the next few years. However, it would be idiotic for them to fight a person in court who has nothing to take.

First, let's start with the bank account. If the collector can find out what bank you use and your account number (from checks or direct deposits the credit card company has in its possession), they can try to take your money with an order from the judge. But you can always close your bank account. When you think about it, you really don't need one. The collector can't get a bank levy if you keep your money hidden in a shoe box under your bed. You can still cash employment checks for a small fee without an actual account at many banks and grocery stores. Or you can even open up an overseas bank account that deals in US dollars. With an offshore account, you will need to make a large initial deposit to open it up, usually a few thousand dollars. After all, those banks need large sums of money to make their own large sums of money. Keep in mind, the bill collectors cannot take your social security, unemployment, or veteran's benefits even if they get a bank levy. Note: if you have a joint account with your spouse, make sure to get separate accounts at different banks. Joint accounts can be seen as joint property in some states, allowing the courts to take all of the money or half of the money in the account, even if most of it is not yours. It's better to be safe than sorry. Google your local state laws regarding bank levies and property liens. There should be plenty of information out there since this type of stuff comes up often in divorce proceedings with unpaid debts.

If you get your wage garnished by the courts, you are pretty much out of luck. But keep in mind, the courts can only take a percentage of your income. You have to be allowed money for food, clothing, heat, and gas for your car. The courts will often take 30 times the minimum wage in your state per week, or 25% of your net income per week. They will choose the lesser amount. So if you make $500 per week, they will probably garnish $125 per week. If you are unemployed, then this option obviously won't work for the bill collectors.

As far as liens on your property, the collector has to first be aware of what property you own. Obviously, if you own a business or house, then the collector will find out. You can always transfer ownership of your property to another family member with a quitclaim deed. Doctors do this often, since they have the potential of getting sued for malpractice. However, if the court thinks you are doing it just to avoid a debt, they could reverse the transfer of ownership. On the other hand, if you owe money and your house is located in a common law state and is listed in your wife's name, then the house is off limits because there is no joint tenancy, or tenancy in common. Collectors can only go after property you own, or property that is owned by both of you, otherwise it is a wrongful lien. Each state can have different laws and exemptions, so check online for the specifics.

Note: if you live in a community property state (Arizona, California, Idaho, Louisiana, Nevada, New Mexico, Texas, Washington, or Wisconsin), then the collector can go after your spouse since the credit card debt was incurred while you were married. In other words, they can put a levy on your spouse' bank account or put a lien against your home, even if you are not the legal owner. Always check with an attorney if you are being sued. Your state might have exemptions which could prevent a spouse's bank levy or lien on a spouse's property. If you live in any of the other states, they are called common law states. Common law means collectors can't go after the property that your spouse owns or the money your spouse earns.

Now it's time to get specific and discuss your plan of attack if you end up getting sued. Remember, your goal is to get the case thrown out of court because the collector didn't follow your court's rules, or the collector didn't prove ownership of the debt, or that the collector didn't prove he is legally able to collect the debt or attorney fees. You want to win this case without ever stepping foot in a court house. So the first part of your case will primarily involve paperwork and some driving to the court house to deliver documents.

1. Read all of your local court's rules. Check Google for your state and county court rules and court forms. If your case ends up in a civil court or small claims court, the rules can limit some of what you want to accomplish. So read over every rule, especially the parts about filing motions, certificates of service, the number of affirmative defenses you can have, and what needs to be notarized. You will need to know all of this before filing motions, or you can get in trouble with the court, and even fined. Learn as much as possible before you get sued, since you only have 20-30 days to answer the complaint. You

have to act immediately, because you want to file your motions before the plaintiff gets a chance to. Also, look online for your state's legal services website regarding debt collection. Some states even have electronic filing services (like www.onelegal.com or www.summonsresponse.com), allowing you to fight the case without ever leaving your home.

2. File a "motion to dismiss the complaint" or "demurrer" before the "answer" if possible. Check your local court rules. If you live in a state that requires a copy of the actual signed contract (instrument) to be included with the summons (Indiana trail rule 9.2), and it's missing, then you can file a motion to dismiss before the answer is filed. In some states, the assignment, or agreement between the debt collector and original creditor should be included, too. If not, then the case could also be dismissed with this motion. Remember, the bill collector has to prove that they legally own the debt, or are acting as lawyers for the original creditor. How much money did a collection agency pay for the debt? This is relevant in many states since it determines actual damages, or how much the plaintiff can actually sue for. The chain of command, and some proof of purchases is required, too. And if the collector is trying to add on additional lawyer's fees, did he include a signed contract which allows for this? Often, tacking on additional fees is only granted if the original agreement says so. Also, if the date of your last payment is past the statute of limitations, then your debt is no longer valid and can be dismissed. Lastly, can the debt collector legally collect debts in your state? If your state requires them to be licensed and bonded and they are not, the case can be dismissed. These claims can also be exhibited in your discovery and motion for summary judgment. Note: if you are unsure if your state allows a motion to dismiss before the answer, then send both the answer and motion to dismiss to the court and the plaintiff. Just be sure that you have clear grounds to file a motion to dismiss. If you are not sure if the argument is legit, put it into your affirmative defenses. Some defendants will file the motion to dismiss in order to delay the proceedings, giving them more time to prepare for the case. However, the plaintiff can always amend their complaint after seeing your motion. So there are different schools of thought on using the motion to dismiss versus the affirmative defense. I believe each can be equally as effective. If you decide to use a motion to dismiss, send a copy to the plaintiff, take one to the court, and keep a copy for yourself.

3. Next, send in your "answer" and "notice of appearance" to the "complaint" and "summons" that you received from the collector's lawyers. The summons tells you where to go to court and when. The notice of appearance tells the plaintiff and the court that you are coming, so no default judgment will be given out. The complaint is a list of all of the bad stuff you did, like breach of contract. It also tells the court how much money the plaintiff wants to collect from you. The answer is your chance to admit to or deny the information contained in each paragraph of the complaint. Plus, you can list all of your "affirmative defenses" which will explain legal reasons why you don't owe this money. Send a copy to the plaintiff, drop off a copy with the court clerk to get stamped, and keep a copy for yourself. Do this with all of your forms or pleadings. Be sure to follow any special rules, like double spacing everything or using special tabs on certain documents. The certificate of service at the end of each document states that you delivered the forms to the plaintiff. Sign it and date it and explain how you mailed out the form (like priority mail with a signature).

4. If a copy of the original signed contract is not included with the plaintiff's summons, an "affidavit of debt" might be. It is a statement from someone claiming to be an expert witness who has knowledge of your account and can prove that you legally own the money. This person is called the affiant. The affiant should be familiar with the original creditor's records of regularly conducted activity. Often, this is not true at all. And in some cases, this "authorized agent of the plaintiff" is clearly a robo-signer, or an employee who just signs his name on thousands of affidavits per month, without knowing a thing about your account. The affiant could be employed by the collection agency, an outside company, or an attorney. The bottom line is, if they are not employed by the original creditor, then their affidavit is garbage! Therefore, you have to challenge this document right away. **You need to challenge the affidavit with a "motion to strike".** Basically, this states that the affidavit is hearsay, and cannot be admitted in court. If that occurs, then the case is pretty much over. If the affidavit is from the original creditor, you can also fight it with a "sworn denial". This is a motion denying the debt, and forcing the expert witness to testify in person. This is expensive and dangerous for the plaintiff to do, since any expert witness can be destroyed in court by asking a few simple questions. How many affidavits of debt does the affiant sign

per day, how much time do they spend on each one, how did they verify the debt, what do they do when there are mistakes with the debt, when and how did they learn about your debt, have they seen the signed contract, where is the signed contract now, what do they know about the original creditor's accounting practices, what did you purchase on the account, where are some examples of your signature on cancelled checks, did you watch every affidavit get notarized? Here is an article by the New York Times which interviewed an affiant who signed 2000 affidavits per day, allowing only 13 seconds for verification and signing. Obviously, there is no way to verify anything in 13 seconds.

http://www.nytimes.com/2010/11/01/business/01debt.html?_r=3&pagewanted=1

So attack the affiant! Send out a copy of the motion to strike to the plaintiff, take one to the court clerk, and keep one for yourself. Remember, you will most likely need three copies of everything.

5. Next comes the "discovery," or exchange of evidence and facts between the plaintiff and defendant. This is where you get to ask the plaintiff questions and try to get him to admit to certain facts that are damaging to the case. The plaintiff will try to do the same thing to you, too. Don't admit to anything, except your name and address. It is the bill collector's responsibility to prove the case, not yours. Again, check your state's rules. You might have to file the discovery with your answer in some courts. There are three main parts to the discovery process: **request for production of documents** (request to see documents, like the original contract), **request for admissions** (request the plaintiff to admit that they don't have evidence, like the contract), and **interrogatories** (questions for the plaintiff to answer about their evidence and procedures of obtaining evidence). Send out the request for production of documents, request for admissions, and notice of service of interrogatories. Each one goes to the plaintiff and court. Keep copies for yourself, too.

6. The "motion to compel" gets filed when the plaintiff refuses to answer your discovery, or refuses to properly answer your discovery questions. This will probably happen. Likewise, you will also refuse to answer their questions in detail. However, the burden of proof lies on their shoulders, not yours. And the court can force them to answer your discovery questions if they are important to the case. If the plaintiff continues to refuse, your requests for admissions will be deemed factual. And that means the end of the lawsuit. Send the motion to compel to the plaintiff and court. Keep a copy for yourself.

7. Answer the plaintiff's discovery (request for documents, admissions, and interrogatories). You will be providing them with nothing except a list of objections like "Defendant objects to interrogatory #5 on the grounds that it is overly broad and unduly burdensome to the extent it seeks information that is not within the current knowledge, possession, custody or control of the Defendant." Watch out for trick questions, or questions asked more than once. They will try to trap you if they can, and even ask YOU for the original contract. Send the plaintiff your discovery answers, and take copies to the court. Keep copies for yourself

7. Motion for summary judgment. When all the information is in and the plaintiff refuses to answer your discovery, you can try to get the case "dismissed with prejudice" (plaintiff can't sue you again), or "dismissed without prejudice" (plaintiff can sue you again). This is where the case should hopefully end. Either the plaintiff will drop the case, the judge will rule in someone's favor with a judgment, or the case will proceed. If the "affidavit of debt" or "sworn account" has not been stricken, then you may need to file a sworn denial to force the affiant to testify in court. You will have to study up on cross examining the affiant who signed the affidavit of debt. You will have to impeach their credibility and prove that their information is hearsay. Some courts look down on a graduated sworn denial, since it doesn't necessarily deny the debt ("I deny the debt, but if it's mine, I deny the amount"), so you might want to use a basic denial. Get the denial notarized (sign it in front of the notary), and file copies with the court and plaintiff.

8. Next comes the bench trial. If the case proceeds to this point and the plaintiff has not withdrawn the case or made you a decent settlement offer, then you will have an actual trial with a judge. If you feel the plaintiff has a strong case, it is still possible to get a lawyer for free, or almost free in many states if you

are broke. Call up some debt collection or bankruptcy lawyers in your area to see if they can offer a flat rate to represent you. Sometimes you can find one that will charge only a few hundred bucks. If you still want to continue to represent yourself, there are some great resources online which can be of great help. www.Yourlegallegup.com offers a debt collection lawsuit ebook coarse for $97. It even comes all the necessary forms and a money back guarantee. You can also check out www.howtoanswerasummons.com for another ebook package that will cut through all of the legal jargon so you can defend yourself in court for only $35. For $14.95 you can go to www.beatdebtcollectors.com and find a great ebook on how to beat the bill collectors in court. All are worth checking out if you are going to end up in courtm and are much cheaper than a lawyer. Sometimes when you show up to court, it's the plaintiff that doesn't show. They want an easy default judgment; they don't want to spend money fighting a case they could lose. There are some free websites online that offer excellent information, and examples of just about every type of court pleading available. Be sure to also check out www.creditinfocenter.com/forums and www.debtorboards.com to learn more about defending yourself in court against debt collectors.

Expect to see dozens of people being sued in court by the same bill collector. Chances are, the plaintiff's counsel might not be prepared to win a single case against any of the debtors in that court room. Often, the collectors only evidence is their "media." This is the information they bought from the original creditor: name, social security, address, and a few statements. Most of the people being sued will admit to owing the debt, and claim that they just can't afford it. Unfortunately, the court could care less. They just lost their case in a matter of minutes.

On the other hand, some debt collectors don't even show up to court and their cases get dismissed. Like I said before, if it is too expensive for the plaintiff to win, they often just give up. Here are the facts. Too many people that are sued refuse to answer the summons or discovery. Therefore, everything the plaintiff claims is often admitted as evidence. A default judgment is quickly granted. In most cases, the debtors are really doing all of the work for the debt collection attorneys. It's easy money. Think about it like this, if you picked 100 random people out of the phone book and sued them for a debt that did not exist, odds are you would probably win a few of the cases and make a net profit. You could easily bring in more money than you spent. Now do that hundreds of thousands of times a year. Pretty soon you can buy off politicians to push even more laws in your favor. Unfortunately, that's the way it is for the collectors in our country. If you don't stand up for yourself once in a while, you will eventually lose your money, your rights, and your freedom.

9. Appeal. If you lose you can always appeal to a higher court by filing a notice of appeal. This can drag the case on for months to years. And you will probably have to file a bond to stop the execution of the judgment. The bottom line is this: if you don't have any money, the plaintiff is not going to get any money anytime soon.

Take a look at this interesting article below. Collection agencies often use computer software to handle their litigation. And these programs can even send out a summons. If you get sued, you may in effect be fighting against a damn machine. What a waste of technology.

http://www.nytimes.com/2010/07/13/business/13collection.html?pagewanted=all

Let's look at examples of the paperwork involved in a debt collection lawsuit. On the next page is an example of a summons that the plaintiff (debt collector) has sent to the defendant. Notice that the court pleadings start out the same way on each document (plaintiff vs. defendant, court name, case number, and pleading title).

You can download all of the court document examples here:

www.snotboards.com/court.zip

If you need help drafting your own legal documents, check out http://www.summonsresponse.com. It's a paid service that will write up your court forms for only $34.95.

```
 1
 2                      DISTRICT COURT FOR THE STATE OF ALASKA
 3
 4    Collection Agency,                      )    Case No.: 1234567
                                              )
 5               Plaintiff,                   )
                                              )    Summons
 6          vs.                               )
                                              )
 7    Joe Smith,                              )
                                              )
 8               Defendant                    )
 9
10
11
12          An action has been or is about to be commenced against the defendant in the above-entitled
13    court by the plaintiff. Plaintiff's claim is stated in the complaint served with this summons. An answer to
14    the complaint which is herewith served upon the defendant, is required within 20 days after service of this
15    summons upon you, exclusive of the day of service. If you fail to do so, judgment by default will be taken
16    against you for the relief demanded in the complaint.
17
18                                            Dated this 1st day of March, 2012
19
20                                            _____
21                                            E. Manning, Esq
                                              Collection Agency
22                                            123 W 10th St.
                                              Fairbanks, AK 99709
23
24
```

The opinions contained in this book are NOT legal advice, and should NOT be interpreted as legal advice, or council. Always consult the services of an attorney whenever you need legal advice.

You can also check out this website for more info on how to read a summons.

http://www.nedap.org/resources/documents/HowtoReadaSummons.pdf

Here is a made up example of what a typical complaint will look like. It states that you defaulted and are being sued for monetary damages due to "breach of contract." That is the plaintiff's cause of action. The plaintiff is named "Collection Agency" and the defendant is "Joe Smith". The lawyer for the collection agency is "E. Manning". The original creditor is "AA Credit Cards". The plaintiff is seeking a judgment for $5000 + $2000 in interest and lawyer fees.

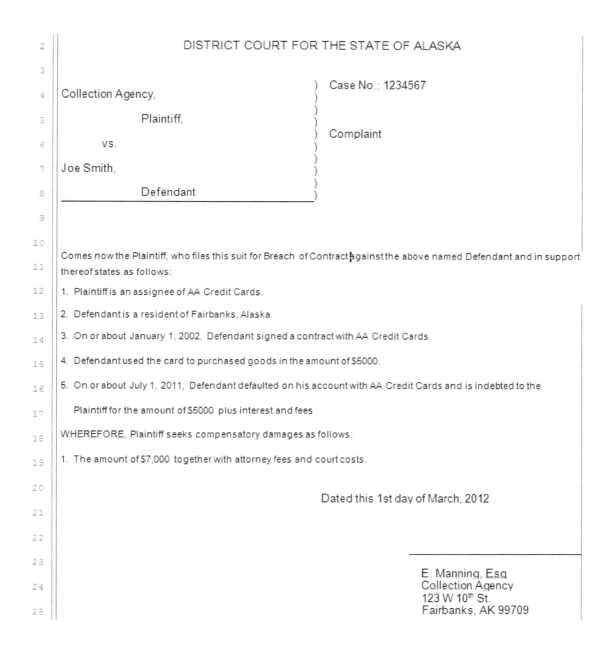

DISTRICT COURT FOR THE STATE OF ALASKA

Collection Agency,

          Plaintiff,

     vs.

Joe Smith,

        Defendant

Case No.: 1234567

Complaint

Comes now the Plaintiff, who files this suit for Breach of Contract against the above named Defendant and in support thereof states as follows:

1. Plaintiff is an assignee of AA Credit Cards.

2. Defendant is a resident of Fairbanks, Alaska.

3. On or about January 1, 2002, Defendant signed a contract with AA Credit Cards.

4. Defendant used the card to purchased goods in the amount of $5000.

5. On or about July 1, 2011, Defendant defaulted on his account with AA Credit Cards and is indebted to the Plaintiff for the amount of $5000 plus interest and fees

WHEREFORE, Plaintiff seeks compensatory damages as follows:

1. The amount of $7,000 together with attorney fees and court costs.

Dated this 1st day of March, 2012

E. Manning, Esq
Collection Agency
123 W 10th St.
Fairbanks, AK 99709

Here is an example of a notice to appear in court. It just lists your name and address so the court and the plaintiff know where to send documents to. The certificate of service at the bottom states that you sent a copy to the plaintiff. All of your court documents need to be sent to the plaintiff's attorney and also taken to the court's clerk to be filed. So make several copies of each one.

DISTRICT COURT FOR THE STATE OF ALASKA

Collection Agency,	)	Case No.: 1234567
Plaintiff,	)	
vs.	)	
Joe Smith,	)	
Defendant	)	Defendant's Notice of Appearance
	)	
	)	
	)	
	)	
	)	

To the Clerk of this Court and all parties of record:

The Defendant, Pro Se, enters an appearance in this action and demands notice of all further proceedings. Any and all notices may be sent to:

Defendant, Pro Se
Your Name
Your Address
City, State, ZIP

CERTIFICATE OF SERVICE

I, Joe Smith, hereby certify that on March 1, 2012, I served copies of the Defendant's Notice of Appearance on the following party by way of U.S. Mail.

E. Manning, Esq
Collection Agency
123 W 10ᵗʰ St.
Fairbanks, AK 99709

_____   _____
Date   Signature

Before we get to the "answer", let's try to get the case thrown out of court. In many states you can file a **"motion to dismiss"** before you send in your answer, or at the same time. If your state requires a copy of the signed contract to be served with the complaint, then the plaintiff's case can be stopped because they didn't comply with a particular trial rule. In Indiana, that would be Trial Rule 9.2. Check online to see what your state's trial rules are. Most states have some type of law requiring the original contract to be produced if "breach of contract" is the basis for the case. If it is not available, an affidavit will take its place as proof. Here are some more reasons for dismissal: "the debt is time barred" (past statute of limitations for your state), or "Plaintiff's counsel has failed to name the real party of interest" (debt collector didn't include assignment papers with the complaint. In other words, the plaintiff has been hired by the original creditor and failed to prove it). Another reason for an early dismissal is "Plaintiff has failed to state a claim for which relief can be granted. Plaintiff has not provided verification of the debt pursuant to the Fair Debt Collection practices Act Title 15 USCA 1692" (You sent them a debt validation letter and they responded with a summons). You cannot get sued if the debt has not been validated. FDCPA law takes precedence. So if they try, you can get the case dismissed and sue them. You can also use "Lack of Standing" (original creditor is not the plaintiff) or "Lack of Personal Jurisdiction" (you weren't properly served). There are many more reasons to dismiss your case. Check online for more reasons under "debt collection motion to dismiss."

Note: when fighting a "common counts" claim, bring up the idea that it is impossible to determine whether a contract actually exists or what precise terms were purportedly breached. The plaintiff's failure to state the terms of the contract, or to attach the agreement, leaves the common counts claim flawed.

Check out the motion to dismiss on the next page along with the memorandum in support of the motion.

You can download all of the court document examples here:

www.snotboards.com/court.zip

DISTRICT COURT FOR THE STATE OF ALASKA

Collection Agency,	) Case No.: 1234567
	)
Plaintiff,	)
	) Motion to Dismiss
vs.	)
	)
Joe Smith,	)
	)
Defendant	)

COMES NOW THE DEFENDANT, Pro Se, and moves the court to dismiss the Plaintiff's claim as follows:

Pursuant to Indiana Trial Rule 9.2 and the Plaintiff's failure to name the real party of interest, Defendant hereby moves the Court to dismiss Plaintiff's Complaint with prejudice. The bases for this Motion are set forth in the accompanying Memorandum.

Dated this 1st day of March, 2012

_____

Defendant
Your Name
Your Address
City, State, ZIP

DISTRICT COURT FOR THE STATE OF ALASKA

Collection Agency,	) Case No.: 1234567
Plaintiff,	)
vs.	) Memorandum in Support of Motion to Dismiss
Joe Smith,	)
Defendant	)

STATEMENT OF FACTS

1. On March 1, 2012, the Plaintiff filed the above complaint with the Clerk of Court in the District Court for the State of Alaska.

2. The Plaintiff is suing the Defendant for the amount of $7000 in regards to an alleged revolving credit card account from the original creditor, AA Credit Cards. Plaintiff provided the Defendant with 12 statement copies from AA Credit Cards dating from January 1, 2006 – January 1, 2007. The last statement before charge off was January 1, 2007.

ARGUMENT

1. The Plaintiffs Council has failed to provide any proof of the alleged debt pursuant to Indiana Trial Rule 9.2. When any pleading is founded on a written instrument, the original, or a copy thereof, must be included in or filed with the pleading.

2. The Plaintiff's counsel has failed to name the real party of interest. The Plaintiff's council did not provide any proof of a relationship between the Collection Agency and AA Credit cards. The Plaintiff's Council has also failed to provide any proof of authority to collect a debt on behalf of AA Credit Cards.

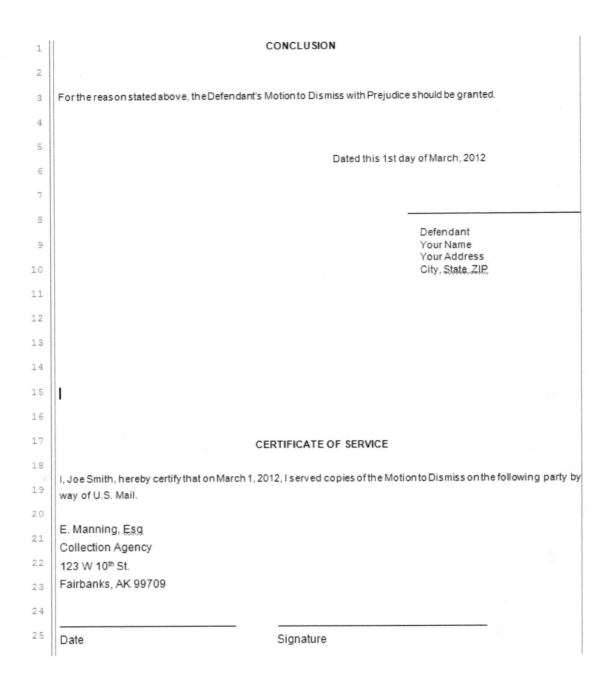

CONCLUSION

For the reason stated above, the Defendant's Motion to Dismiss with Prejudice should be granted.

Dated this 1st day of March, 2012

_____

Defendant
Your Name
Your Address
City, State, ZIP

CERTIFICATE OF SERVICE

I, Joe Smith, hereby certify that on March 1, 2012, I served copies of the Motion to Dismiss on the following party by way of U.S. Mail.

E. Manning, Esq
Collection Agency
123 W 10th St.
Fairbanks, AK 99709

_____   _____
Date   Signature

Next comes your answer to the complaint. Basically in this form you will deny everything except your name or residence, since it is the plaintiff's job to prove the case to the court. Remember, you do not have sufficient knowledge because the plaintiff has not given you ample proof of anything! You will also include a Certificate of Service, which is a sentence or two which states that you mailed a copy of your court forms to the plaintiff. Another copy gets filed with the court clerk, and you will keep a copy for yourself.

DISTRICT COURT FOR THE STATE OF ALASKA

Collection Agency,
    Plaintiff,

  vs.

Joe Smith,
    Defendant

) Case No.: 1234567
)
)
)
)
) Answer, Affirmative Defenses
)
)
)
)
)

COMES NOW THE DEFENDANT, Pro Se, and answers the Plaintiff's claim as follows:

1. Defendant denies the allegations contained in Paragraph 1 of the Complaint as Defendant is without information or knowledge sufficient to form an opinion as to the truth of the assignment.

2. Defendant admits the statements contained in paragraph number 2.

3. Defendant denies the statements in paragraph 3 and is without knowledge of whether or not the original account holder issued credit to the Defendant and requests Plaintiff to provide proof.

4. Defendant denies the allegations in paragraph 4 and lacks knowledge as to how much money, if any is due and asks the Plaintiff to provide proof.

5. Defendant denies the allegations contained in Paragraph 5 as there never been any agreement or contract between the Plaintiff and Defendant.

Affirmative Defenses

1. The Plaintiff failed to state a cause of action upon which relief can be granted.

2. Plaintiff's Complaint fails to allege a valid assignment of debt.

3. The action is barred by the Statute of Frauds.

4. The action is barred by Lack of Privity.

5. The Plaintiff has not proven the debt is valid or the amount is accurate. The Plaintiff must prove that the principal, interest, collection costs, and attorneys fees are all correct, agreed to in your contract, and lawfully charged.

6. The Plaintiff has not proven that they are authorized and licensed to collect claims for others in the State of Indiana.

7. The action is barred by Failure of Consideration.

8. Plaintiff is barred from collecting interest and any amount unless it is expressly authorized by the agreement creating the alleged debt.

9. Plaintiff's damages are limited to actual damages, or actual cost paid by the Plaintiff to purchase the debt.

10. The action is barred by the Statute of Limitations.

11. Defendant reserves the right to add additional Affirmative Defenses at a later date.

WHEREFORE, the defendant asks the Court for judgment: dismissing the complaint herein with prejudice

CERTIFICATE OF SERVICE

I, Joe Smith, hereby certify that on March 1, 2012, I served copies of the Answer and Affirmative Defenses on the following party by way of U.S. Mail.

E. Manning, Esq
Collection Agency
123 W 10th St.
Fairbanks, AK 99709

_____   _____
Date   Signature

Let's talk about the specific **Answers** to this complaint. These are just some of the answers which can be used. If you look online, you can probably come up with dozens of answers that will pertain to your specific case. The main goal here is to prove that the plaintiff has not proven any of their allegations.

Complaint #1 will be denied because the collection agency usually does not provide any proof of a contractual agreement between the collection agency and the original creditor. How do you know that they are even working for them?

Complaint #2 can be admitted since they know your address.

Complaint #3 will be denied because there is no proof that you signed a legal agreement with the original creditor. Use this answer unless the plaintiff includes a copy of the **original signed contract** with the summons and complaint. And if the Plaintiff refers to the "cardholder agreement" that you signed anywhere in the complaint, they need to attach it to the complaint and bring it into evidence. Even if they use a general claim that your billing statements show proof of an implied agreement under the "Common Counts" claim, you still need to see what the agreement or contract they are referencing actually says. To fight this, you need to ask for a complete itemized list of all charges in your discovery (request for production of documents), or submit a "Bill of Particulars" if your state allows it. Use a motion to compel when the Plaintiff fails to answer. When the Plaintiff still refuses to answer, file a motion to dismiss or motion for summary judgment. On the other hand, if the Plaintiff is suing for "Breach of Contract", then the original signed contract or affidavit of debt must be present in most courts.

Complaint #4 will be denied because the plaintiff has not provided any real proof that you owe $5000 to the original creditor or collection agency. Just because they say it, doesn't mean it is true.

Complaint #5 will be denied because there is no proof that you legally owe the collection agency any money. There is no apparent contract between the plaintiff and defendant.

The next section is the **Affirmative Defenses**. These are the legal reasons why the case should be thrown out of court. Again, you can check online and find dozens of defenses which you can use in your specific case.

Affirmative Defense #1 is used because the plaintiff did not provide proof of the original signed contract with the complaint.

Affirmative Defense #2 is used because the plaintiff did not provide a contract or agreement between the original creditor and the collection agency, often referred to as "the chain of custody."

Affirmative Defense #3 is used because under contract law, a signed contract is required and has not been produced by the plaintiff.

Affirmative Defense #4 is used since there is no contact between the Plaintiff and the Collection Agency. You don't legally owe them money, unless the original signed contract from the original creditor says "you owe the hired assignee of the original creditor for debt if it goes into default." But the original signed contract needs to be produced for that.

Affirmative Defense #5 is used because accurate accounting of the debt is needed in order to determine the amount owed. You need to see a breakdown of all interest and fees, too.

Affirmative Defense #6 can be used if your state requires collection agencies to be licensed and bonded. Check online for your state's rules.

Affirmative Defense #7 is used because there is no sale of goods or deal of any kind between the plaintiff and defendant.

Affirmative Defense #8 is used if the plaintiff adds on fees to the debt that is owed. This is only allowed if stated in the original signed contract from the original creditor.

Affirmative Defense #9 allows the plaintiff to sue for actual damages. So if he paid 2 cents on the dollar for the debt, his damages are 2 cents on the dollar. Plus, these damages are caused by the plaintiff's own actions, since he decided to buy the debt from the original creditor.

Affirmative Defense #10 is used if the debt is past the statute of limitations in your state, and is no longer valid.

In the last line, the defendant is stating the case should be dropped with prejudice, meaning this case cannot be filed again by the plaintiff. You can probably find another 50 affirmative defenses online, so be sure to search for "debt collection affirmative defenses" on Google.

Note: if the summons and complaint came with an "affidavit of debt" instead of a copy of the original contract, then you must attack its validity with a "motion to strike the affidavit of debt." The motion to strike is going to be one of your most solid weapons. It can kill a case fast if the affidavit is not deemed admissible. Here is probably what will happen if you end up getting sued by a debt collector. More often than not, the original contract no longer exists, or is no longer obtainable, so the collector needs an affidavit of debt in order to get a default judgment. It is a signed statement by an employee who declares under oath that you owe the debt. This employee often knows nothing about your account, except the amount due. And if they are not an employee of the original creditor, then there is no way they can be considered an expert. Often the affidavit doesn't even have your name or account number on it, and there are no sworn or certified copies of documents provided as proof. Sometimes it is not even notarized, and the amounts are incorrect. Furthermore, how did the affiant verify the debt? These affidavits are nothing more than junk, and many courts tend to agree. There is plenty of case law on this subject.

In the case of **Glarum v. LaSalle Bank National Association**, the affiant couldn't determine who entered the data into the system, could not verify that the figures were correct, and was not familiar with the procedures used by the supplier of the data. In other words, the affidavit was garbage.

Check out the motion to strike example below.

	DISTRICT COURT FOR THE STATE OF ALASKA

Collection Agency,   )   Case No.: 1234567

           Plaintiff,   )

       vs.   )

Joe Smith,   )

           Defendant   )   Motion to Strike Affidavit of Debt

)

)

)

)

_____

COMES NOW THE DEFENDANT, Pro Se, and requests that the court strike the Plaintiff's Affidavit of Debt.

1. Plaintiff has submitted into evidence an Affidavit of Debt.

2. The Affiant writing the Affidavit of Debt has not explained how the credit card records of the Plaintiff came into his possession.

3. The Affiant writing the Affidavit of Debt has not claimed to have any personal knowledge of how records are kept at the original creditor, AA Credit Cards. **Palisades Collection, LLC. v Gonzalez (2005)**

4. At no time was the Affiant of the Affidavit of Debt present to witness any alleged acts or creation of the debt.

5. The Affiant writing the Affidavit of Debt has never been employed by AA Credit Cards and does not have personal knowledge of how AA Credit Card's records are prepared or maintained and is unqualified to testify as to the truth of the information contained in the Affidavit of Debt.

6. The Affiant of Debt has not provided any sworn or certified documents to prove the validity of the debt. **Luke vs. Unifund CCR Partners (2007)**

1	
2	CERTIFICATE OF SERVICE
3	I, Joe Smith, hereby certify that on March 1, 2012, I served copies of the Motion to Strike Affidavit of Debt on the
4	following party by way of U.S. Mail.
5	
6	E. Manning, Esq
7	Collection Agency
8	123 W 10th St.
9	Fairbanks, AK 99709
10	Date Signature
11	
12	
13	

You should add case law to your pleadings to help prove your arguments. There are quite a bit of cases out there where the bogus affidavits were stricken down by the court. The Debtorboards website has tons of case law to read through and use in your affirmative defenses, motions, and discovery. Write down the case names that are pertinent to your case. Try to use case law from your state if it exists. You can, however, use other state's case law if needed.

http://www.debtorboards.com/index.php?board=88.0

If your state requires a memorandum in support of your motion to strike, then you can add your case law to that document instead. A memorandum is just a memo with facts or other information that can help the judge to make a decision in your favor. In this case, the memorandum will have arguments and case law proving why affidavits have not been deemed admissible in court. The judge's decisions are your proof. You can use a simple legal format which is similar to the motion for summary judgment. It has material facts, legal arguments, and a conclusion. Always check your local court rules to see if memorandums or affidavits are required when pleading or filing motions.

DISTRICT COURT FOR THE STATE OF ALASKA

Collection Agency,

        Plaintiff,

     vs.

Joe Smith,

        Defendant

Case No.: 1234567

Memorandum in Support of Defendant's Motion to Strike Plaintiff's Affidavit of Debt

COMES NOW THE DEFENDANT, Pro Se, and files this Memorandum in Support of Defendant's Motion to Strike Plaintiff's Affidavit of Debt as follows:

Statement of Material Facts

1. The Plaintiff's Affidavit of Debt has failed to provide proof of debt, or an intimate knowledge of the creation of the debt.

2. Plaintiff's Affidavit is hearsay and presumes facts not in evidence.

Legal Arguments

1. In face of answer denying all allegations of the complaint, an affidavit containing statement by officer of plaintiff that the allegations of the complaint are insufficient to support motion for summary judgment. **Nour v. All State Pipe Supply Co. 487 So.2d 1204 (1986)**

2. The Affiant writing the Affidavit of Debt has not claimed to have any personal knowledge of how records are kept at the original creditor, AA Credit Cards. **Palisades Collection, LLC. v Gonzalez (2005)**

3. The Affiant of Debt has not provided any sworn or certified documents to prove the validity of the debt. **Luke v.s. Unifund CCR Partners (2007)**

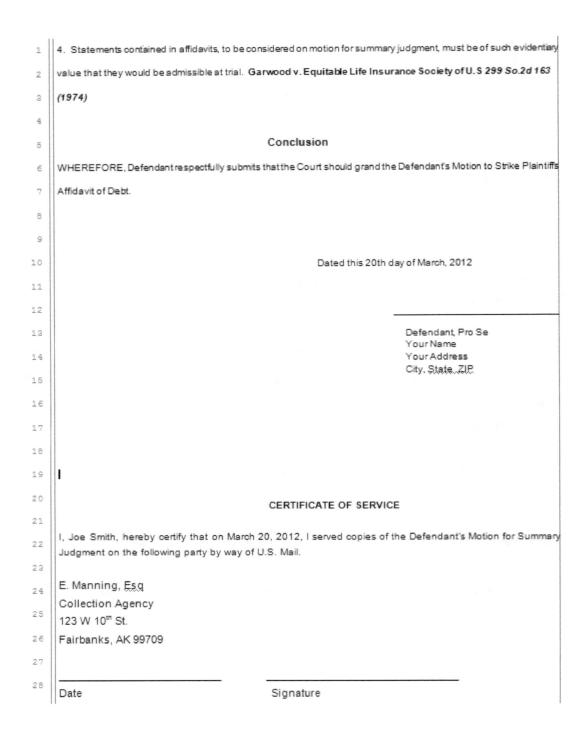

1 4. Statements contained in affidavits, to be considered on motion for summary judgment, must be of such evidentiary

2 value that they would be admissible at trial. Garwood v. Equitable Life Insurance Society of U.S 299 So.2d 163

3 *(1974)*

4

5   Conclusion

6 WHEREFORE, Defendant respectfully submits that the Court should grand the Defendant's Motion to Strike Plaintiffs

7 Affidavit of Debt.

8

9

10   Dated this 20th day of March, 2012

11

12   _____

13   Defendant, Pro Se
                                               Your Name
14   Your Address
                                               City, State, ZIP
15

16

17

18

19 I

20   CERTIFICATE OF SERVICE

21

22 I, Joe Smith, hereby certify that on March 20, 2012, I served copies of the Defendant's Motion for Summary
    Judgment on the following party by way of U.S. Mail.
23

24 E. Manning, Esq
    Collection Agency
25 123 W 10th St.
26 Fairbanks, AK 99709

27

28 _____   _____
    Date   Signature

Next, comes the discovery process, or the evidence gathering process. This is where each side gets to ask for information to prove their case. This is basically the trial, but it is located on paper instead of inside a courtroom. When all of the evidence is out in the open, you can motion for the judge to make a summary judgment in your favor. Your goal during this phase of the trial is to discredit the Plaintiff and gather information to support your defenses. You need to prove that the plaintiff doesn't have the proper documentation, proper expertise, or legal standing to bring a lawsuit against you. You also want the court to know that the plaintiff routinely violates the FDCPA through case law examples, which you can verify on Justia.com. Many of the big collection agencies that will come after you will have plenty of dirty laundry aired online. You can bet that they have been sued for breaking the law. Finally, at the very least cause the Plaintiff's legal fees to add up quickly. $150/hour can quickly turn into thousands of dollars defending a case that they could lose. It's much easier for them to cut their losses and go after someone who doesn't send in their notice of appearance or show up to court.

After you send in your discovery requests, you will notice that the Plaintiff probably won't truthfully answer your questions, so you will have to file a "motion to compel" with the court, forcing them to answer. Since the burden of proof is solely on the Plaintiff, you do not need to give them any facts or information that will hurt your case.

The first part of discovery is the request for **production of documents**. You need to see all of their evidence and notes, including all contracts between all interested parties. Does the original signed contract exist? Does the Plaintiff really own the debt, and how much did they pay for it? How was the debt created? Who works for the Plaintiff? Since most collection agencies have such a high turnover rate (some at 50% per year), it's more likely that their workers will be less skilled and be more apt to make costly mistakes. Maybe the employee that signed the Affidavit of Debt (affiant) works for the collection agency and not the original creditor. And maybe he or she pumps out hundreds of affidavits per week? Obviously, they can't be an account expert if no time has been allotted to verify the accuracy of the affidavits. If the plaintiff answers your requests, then the discovery process has now made your case much easier to win. Odds are, you will probably have to force the answers out of them if they don't drop the case.

Feel free to add definitions to your discovery forms if needed. The last thing you want to happen is the plaintiff denying your request because the question was vague and not specific. If you use a term like creditor, add a definition to clarify who the creditor is. Or include the clarification in the discovery request. Just make sure nothing is confusing.

The next part is **the request for admissions**. Here is the theory behind admissions. If both sides agree on certain issues, it will save time in the courtroom since those points are not in dispute and considered to be facts. If nothing is in dispute, then the case is ready for a judgment, since there is nothing to argue about. However, it is unlikely both sides will agree to much, if anything. With that being said, during this phase you still want to try to get the Plaintiff to admit to certain facts that will help your case. If the plaintiff won't agree to your admissions, then they need to answer why not.

The last part of the discovery process is the **interrogatories**. These are the written questions that you get to ask the plaintiff under oath in order to gather more information. Presenting the plaintiff with interrogatories is kind of like being a trial lawyer on paper. And like a good trial lawyer, you will use these questions to tear down the plaintiff's case, piece by piece. Destroy his credibility and the chain of custody for any documents he has. Even if the debt is legitimate, if the plaintiff is not qualified or prepared to answer tough questions, then his legal arguments won't be believed. For example, when was the debt created, or when was the original contract executed? What's the last charge on the account? Do the numbers match your credit report numbers? If the plaintiff doesn't know this stuff, how can he verify the debt? How does the affiant verify the affidavit of debt? What documents does he or she use, and where do they come from? And where did they come from before that? Odds are, the affiant doesn't verify anything and uses very little information to make an expert opinion on the validity of the debt. Or how much did the collection agency pay for the debt? If they only paid $100 for the debt, why are they suing for $7000 in damages for breach of contract? What are their real damages? Or maybe the plaintiff does not even own the debt. How were the billing statements obtained by the plaintiff? Are they re-prints made recently, or actual photocopies of the real bill? They might not be admissible. So, the more information you can get out of them, the more likely they are going to mess up and lose credibility. Take a look at the link below for some example questions that can destroy an affiant in a matter of seconds.

http://stopforeclosurefraud.com/2011/08/16/robo-affidavit-class-action-settles-for-5-2-million-midland-funding-v-brent/

Bear in mind, most states limit the number of interrogatories you can ask to 25-35 questions, so make sure you pick ones that help prove your affirmative defenses. There are hundreds of interrogatories online, so you should be able to find the right ones to fit your case. In the made up example I listed, the affidavit of debt was not removed by the court after a motion to strike was filed. In that case, you simply attack the affiant in the discovery process. Do a Google search online for debt collection interrogatories and be sure to read your local court rules regarding the discovery process.

You can download all of the court document examples here:

www.snotboards.com/court.zip

DISTRICT COURT FOR THE STATE OF ALASKA

Collection Agency,	) Case No.: 1234567
Plaintiff,	)
vs.	)
Joe Smith,	)
Defendant	) Request for Production of Documents
	)
	)
	)
	)
	)

_____

Please answer the following Discovery requests as required by the Alaska Rules of Civil Procedure. The Plaintiff shall produce and permit the Defendant to inspect and copy the following documents subject to the set of instructions set forth below:

Definitions

1. The Plaintiff is The Collection Agency, its employees, attorneys, officers, and all others who have collected information on behalf of The Collection Agency.

2. The Defendant is Joe Smith.

3. The contract, or agreement, or account refers to the alleged signed contract between Joe Smith and AA Credit Cards.

4. The assignment is the bill of sale, all assignment documents, and complete chain of custody between AA Credit Cards and the Plaintiff.

5. The application is the alleged document submitted by the Defendant to AA Credit Cards for the purpose of opening a revolving credit account.

6. The debt is the alleged debt concerning the matter which is herein in controversy.

7. The account is the alleged revolving credit card account concerning the matter which is herein in controversy.

8. The Affiant is the individual who swears to the Affidavit of Debt that was submitted by the Plaintiff.

Request for Production of Documents

1. The actual signed credit card contract upon which your Complaint is based on that states interest rate, grace period, finance charge, terms of repayment, and state laws that the agreement and account are governed by. Also include each subsequent revised agreement or addendum.

2. Plaintiff's entire file concerning the matter which is herein in controversy, including all records, reports, memoranda relating to this disputed account and all other sources of information, such as locations at which related information is located or accessible.

3. All invoices and statements created by the Plaintiff concerning the matter which is herein in controversy.

4. All invoices and statements created by the AA Credit Cards concerning the matter which is herein in controversy.

5. All contracts, agreements, assignments, and memoranda of agreements between AA Credit Cards and the Defendant concerning the matter which is herein in controversy.

6. All contracts, agreements, assignments, and memoranda of agreements between AA Credit Cards and the Plaintiff concerning the matter which is herein in controversy.

7. All contracts, agreement, assignments, memoranda or other means of demonstrating that the Plaintiff has the authority and is legally entitled to collect on the alleged debt in the state of Alaska.

8. An itemized account of all purchases and transactions that the Defendant made on the alleged account with AA Credit Cards, which should include complete and accurate history of the interest charged. Show the exact dates those interest rates changed, and explain the exact method of amortization.

9. All letters, enclosures, envelopes, memoranda used by the Plaintiff in their collection efforts against the Defendant.

10. Copies of all litigation filed against the Plaintiff for alleged violations of the Fair Debt Collection Practices Act.

11. A list of all of the Plaintiff's employees, including attorneys, engaged in the collection of debt concerning the matter which is herein in controversy. List their positions, responsibilities, and duration of time that they have been employed by the Plaintiff.

12. All operation manuals, training memoranda, videos, tapes, or similar documents used by the Plaintiff for employee training.

13. All documents, reports, and memoranda relating to the Plaintiffs association with consumer reporting agencies.

14. Copies of all reports, documents, and exhibits that the Plaintiff or any other witness proposes to call at trial concerning the matter which is herein in controversy.

15. Copies of all amendments to the alleged agreement between the Defendant and AA Credit Cards.

CERTIFICATE OF SERVICE

I, Joe Smith, hereby certify that on March 1, 2012, I served copies of the Request for Production of Documents on the following party by way of U.S. Mail.

E. Manning, Esq
Collection Agency
123 W 10th St.
Fairbanks, AK 99709

_____   _____

Date   Signature

DISTRICT COURT FOR THE STATE OF ALASKA

Collection Agency,	) Case No.: 1234567
Plaintiff,	)
vs.	)
Joe Smith,	)
Defendant	) Request for Admissions
	)
	)
	)
	)
_____	)

Pursuant to The Federal Rules of Civil Procedure, the Defendant requests that the Plaintiff under oath admits or denies the truth of the following statements, subject to the set of instructions set forth below. If the Plaintiff refuses to acknowledge any of the admissions as being true, please explain why the statement has been denied.

Definitions

1. The Plaintiff is The Collection Agency, its employees, attorneys, officers, and all others who have collected information on behalf of The Collection Agency.

2. The Defendant is Joe Smith.

3. The contract, or agreement, or account refers to the alleged signed contract between Joe Smith and AA Credit Cards.

4. The assignment is the bill of sale, all assignment documents, and complete chain of custody between AA Credit Cards and the Plaintiff.

5. The application is the alleged document submitted by the Defendant to AA Credit Cards for the purpose of opening a revolving credit account.

6. The debt is the alleged debt owed by the Defendant.

7. The account is the alleged revolving credit card account concerning the matter which is herein in controversy.

8. The Affiant is the individual who swears to the Affidavit of Debt that was submitted by the Plaintiff.

Request for Admissions

1. Please admit the Plaintiff is in the business of collecting consumer debts and is a debt collector as defined in 15 U.S.C. 1692a(6).

2. The Plaintiff was not assigned AA Credit Card's obligations under the purchase agreement.

3. The Plaintiff is not licensed to collect debts in the state of Alaska.

4. The Plaintiff does not know the date of execution of the alleged agreement between AA Credit Cards and the Defendant.

5. The Plaintiff does not have a signed contract or application showing that an account with AA Credit Cards was established in the Defendant's name.

6. The Plaintiff has no merchant receipts showing charges that were incurred on an account in the Defendant's name.

7. The Plaintiff has not proven that the alleged debt was accurately calculated.

8. The Plaintiff purchases portfolios of defaulted debts in their course of business.

9. The Plaintiff is not the original creditor of the alleged debt described in the Complaint.

10. The Plaintiff regularly purchases defaulted debts at a small percentage of their original balance in their course of business.

11. The Plaintiff has never exchanged goods or services with the Defendant.

12. The Plaintiff has not validated the debt according to the Fair Debt Collection Practices Act.

13. The Plaintiff does not have standing to initiate a lawsuit to collect the alleged debt from the Defendant.

14. The Plaintiff is not an injured party in this lawsuit. If denied, explain the amount of the loss sustained.

15. The Affiant who signed the Affidavit of Debt is an employee of The Collection Agency.

16. The Plaintiff has been sued in the past for violating the Fair Debt Collection Practices Act.

17. AA Credit Cards is unaware of any legal action that is being taken by the Plaintiff concerning the matter which is

herein in controversy.

18. The Plaintiff does not have any cancelled checks or other proof that payments were made on the alleged account with AA Credit Cards.

CERTIFICATE OF SERVICE

I, Joe Smith, hereby certify that on March 1, 2012, I served copies of the Request for Admissions on the following party by way of U.S. Mail.

E. Manning, Esq
Collection Agency
123 W 10ᵗʰ St.
Fairbanks, AK 99709

_____   _____
Date   Signature

The opinions contained in this book are NOT legal advice, and should NOT be interpreted as legal advice, or council. Always consult the services of an attorney whenever you need legal advice.

DISTRICT COURT FOR THE STATE OF ALASKA

Collection Agency,	) Case No.: 1234567
Plaintiff,	)
vs.	)
Joe Smith,	)
Defendant	) Interrogatories
	)
	)
	)
	)
	)

Pursuant to The Federal Rules of Civil Procedure, the Defendant requests that the Plaintiff under oath answers the Interrogatories, subject to the set of instructions set forth below.

Definitions

1. The Plaintiff is The Collection Agency, its employees, attorneys, officers, and all others who have collected information on behalf of The Collection Agency.

2. The Defendant is Joe Smith.

3. The contract, or agreement, or account refers to the alleged signed contract between Joe Smith and AA Credit Cards.

4. The assignment is the bill of sale, all assignment documents, and complete chain of custody between AA Credit Cards and the Plaintiff.

5. The application is the alleged document submitted by the Defendant to AA Credit Cards for the purpose of opening up a revolving credit account.

6. The debt is the alleged debt owed by the Defendant.

7. The account is the alleged revolving credit card account concerning the matter which is herein in controversy.

8. The Affiant is the individual who swears to the Affidavit of Debt that was submitted by the Plaintiff.

Interrogatories

1. Is the Plaintiff an assignee of AA Credit Cards, or is the Plaintiff an assignee of another debt collection agency?

2. Does the Plaintiff use any other names to identify its organization? Please list each one along with the location of registration.

3. Identify each person answering the Request for Admissions and Interrogatories. What is their title and how many years have they worked for their current employer.

4. List in detail how the billing statements from AA Credit Cards were obtained and transferred to the Plaintiff.

5. State the factual basis for each claim you will assert in this legal action against the Defendant.

6. When did the Defendant open up the alleged credit card account with AA Credit Cards?

7. On what date did the Defendant become indebted to the Plaintiff for $7000?

8. On what date did the Defendant default on the alleged account with AA Credit Cards?

9. Please list the purchases that were made on this account and the dates that they were made.

9. State the names, job titles, and employee identification numbers of the Plaintiff's employees who engage in the collection of consumer debt.

10. State the names, job titles, and employee identification numbers of the Plaintiff's employees who have resigned or been terminated within the last 12 months.

11. State the number of collection notices, similar to those sent to the Defendant, that were mailed out by the Plaintiff within the last 12 months.

11. List all procedures the Plaintiff used to verify the accuracy of the alleged debt owed to AA Credit Cards.

12. Identify all present and past contracts between the Plaintiff and AA Credit Cards.

13. Does the Plaintiff file or retain attorneys to file lawsuits to collect consumer debts?

14. Who signed the Affidavit of Debt? What is the Affiant's name, job title, and work experience history?

14. List the basis of knowledge for the Affiant who signed the Affidavit of Debt. Describe his/her education. Where did he/she attend college? When did the Affiant graduate? What type of degree did the Affiant's receive?

15. How many Affidavits of Debt does the Affiant sign per day? How many does he/she sign per week?

16. List all procedures that the Affiant used to verify the accuracy of the alleged debt owed to AA Credit Cards. What documents were given to the Affiant for verification of this alleged debt? Were these same documents sent to the Defendant with the Complaint?

17. Does the Affiant have authorized access to original signed documents at AA Credit Cards? If so, list the individuals who gave the Affiant such authorization?

18. Who is the Affiant employed by? Identify the entity that issues his/her paycheck.

19. Does the Affiant use a computer to fill out Affidavits of Debt? How did the Affiant obtain the name and amount of debt owed by the Defendant? Describe this process in detail.

20. Has the Affiant viewed the alleged contract between the Defendant and AA credit Cards? If so, what amendment terms were written on the contract?

21. How does the Affiant know that the documents provided to him/her for verification of a debt are accurate and authentic? How much time does the Affiant spend verifying a debt before signing an Affidavit of Debt

22. Please describe the Affiant's process for correction of errors while reviewing documents related to consumer debt.

23. Has the Affiant ever been disciplined or written up in the current or previous workplace?

24. How do Affidavits of Debt get notarized by the Affiant? Does the Affiant personally take the Affidavits of Debt to the Notary to be notarized? Does the Affiant watch the Notary authenticate each affidavit?

25. Is the Notary who signed the Affidavit of Debt in this case employed by The Collection Agency? If not, then by whom?

CERTIFICATE OF SERVICE

I, Joe Smith, hereby certify that on March 1, 2012, I served copies of the Interrogatories on the following party by way of U.S. Mail.

E. Manning, Esq

Collection Agency

123 W 10th St.

Fairbanks, AK 99709

_____   _____

Date   Signature

On the next page are some examples of a sworn denial and graduated sworn denial. You can use this if the affidavit of debt has not been removed with your motion to strike. Basically these documents state that the debt is not yours, or that the amount of the debt is wrong, so the debt is not yours. This will force the affiant to testify about the validity of the affidavit, which is expensive and dangerous for the plaintiff to do, since affiants in the credit card industry don't really validate anything. I prefer the basic denial because it states that you don't owe the debt, but doesn't say why. So even if the court finds that you owe the debt, if the amount is incorrect, you don't owe the debt due to errors in accounting, which the affiant never checked. For example, if you owe me $100, and I sue for $99.99, the case can get dismissed due to my error in accounting. The debt can also be incorrect because of the attorney fees and interest that were added to the balance. They are not allowed to add fees unless the original signed contract says so. In some states, you can also request a bill of particulars, which will require complete accounting for the debt. Remember, the sworn denial needs to be notarized, which proves that you actually signed the document in front of a notary. Any type of sworn statement needs notarization.

You can download all of the court document examples here:

www.snotboards.com/court.zip

DISTRICT COURT FOR THE STATE OF ALASKA

Collection Agency,   )   Case No.: 1234567
                    Plaintiff,   )
          vs.   )
Joe Smith,   )
                    Defendant   )   Sworn Denial
)
)
)
)
)
_____

Comes the defendant, Joe Smith, and for plea denies that he is liable to the plaintiff in this case for the amount sued for on the sworn account herein, and demands strict proof thereof. Subscribed and sworn to before me this 4th day of May, 2012.

                                        _____
                                        Defendant, Pro Se
                                        Your Name
                                        Your Address
                                        City, State, ZIP

_____
Notary Public for Alaska
My commission expires
___ Day of _____, 2___.

CERTIFICATE OF SERVICE

I, Joe Smith, hereby certify that on May 4, 2012, I served copies of the Sworn Denial on the following party by way of U.S. Mail.

E. Manning, Esq.
Collection Agency
123 W 10th St.
Fairbanks, AK 99709

_____   _____
Date   Signature

After you have sent in your discovery requests, you will probably be receiving the plaintiff's discovery in the mail. Deny everything except the obvious. Remember, it is the plaintiff's job to prove the case. Watch out for trick questions, like did you make a settlement offer with the original creditor, or is the amount that you are being sued for correct? Don't admit to anything, except your name and address. Here is a sample response to the plaintiff's interrogatories. Include the plaintiff's questions with your response.

DISTRICT COURT FOR THE STATE OF ALASKA

Collection Agency,	)	Case No.: 1234567
Plaintiff,	)	
vs.	)	
Joe Smith,	)	
Defendant	)	Defendant's Response to Plaintiff's Interrogatories
	)	
	)	
	)	
	)	

_____

Pursuant to The Federal Rules of Civil Procedure, the Defendant hereby responds to the Plaintiff's Interrogatories as follows.

Interrogatory #1: Please identify the person by name and address who answered these interrogatories.

Response: Defendant, Pro Se
Your Name
Address
City, State Zip

Interrogatory #2: What is the Defendant's social security number?

Response: The Defendant objects to interrogatory #2 as it is overly invasive of the Defendant's privacy rights, and not relevant to this case, and is not reasonably calculated to lead to the discovery of admissible evidence.

Interrogatory #3: What is the Defendant's bank account number?

Response: The Defendant objects to interrogatory #3 as it is overly invasive of the Defendant's privacy rights, and not relevant to this case, and is not reasonably calculated to lead to the discovery of admissible evidence.

Interrogatory #4: What was the date of the Defendant's last payment made to AA Credit Cards?

Response: Defendant objects to interrogatory #4 on the grounds that it is overly broad and unduly burdensome to the extent it seeks information that is not within the current knowledge, possession, custody or control of the Defendant. Without waiving the Defendant's objection, the Defendant has no knowledge if the amount on the alleged account he is being sued upon is the amount owed.

Interrogatory #5: If the Defendant owes a lesser amount that stated on the Complaint, please state the correct amount.

Response: Defendant objects to interrogatory #5 on the grounds that it is overly broad and unduly burdensome to the extent it seeks information that is not within the current knowledge, possession, custody or control of the Defendant. Without waiving the Defendant's objection, the Defendant has no knowledge if the amount on the alleged account he is being sued upon is the amount owed.

CERTIFICATE OF SERVICE

I, Joe Smith, hereby certify that on March 1, 2012, I served copies of the Defendant's Response to Plaintiff's Interrogatories on the following party by way of U.S. Mail.

E. Manning, Esq
Collection Agency
123 W 10ᵗʰ St.
Fairbanks, AK 99709

_____   _____

Date   Signature

Here is an example of the Defendants response to the plaintiff's request for documents. They are going to try to bait you into giving up evidence for their case. They also want to find out all of your banking information in case they get a default judgment. Only give them your name and address, nothing else.

DISTRICT COURT FOR THE STATE OF ALASKA

Collection Agency,	)	Case No.: 1234567
Plaintiff,	)	
vs.	)	
Joe Smith,	)	
Defendant	)	Defendant's Response to Plaintiff's Request for
	)	Production of Documents
	)	
	)	
	)	
	)	

Pursuant to The Federal Rules of Civil Procedure, the Defendant hereby responds to the Plaintiff's Request for Documents as follows.

Request #1: Please provide examples of cancelled checks used to pay on this debt.

Response: Defendant objects to this Request on the grounds that he has no such documents in its possession, custody or control. This request should be accessible to the Plaintiff from the Plaintiff's own files, from documents or information already in Plaintiff's possession.

Request #2: Please provide examples of all communication between the Defendant and AA Credit Cards.

Response: Defendant objects to this Request on the grounds that he has no such documents in its possession, custody or control. This request should be accessible to the Plaintiff from the Plaintiff's own files, from documents or information already in Plaintiff's possession.

Request #3: Produce all documentation the Defendant plans to use to support his defense.

Response: Defendant objects to this Request on the grounds that the Plaintiff is seeking information that is premature, given that the parties are in the midst of discovery and pertinent documents have not yet been produced by the Plaintiff.

Request #4: Please provide your social security number.

Response: Defendant objects to Plaintiff's Request on the grounds that the Plaintiff seeks to require disclosure of confidential information. This Request is not reasonably calculated to lead to the discovery of admissible evidence.

Request #4: Please provide proof of employment.

Response: Defendant objects to this Request on the grounds that it is vague, overbroad and unduly burdensome.

CERTIFICATE OF SERVICE

I, Joe Smith, hereby certify that on March 1, 2012, I served copies of the Defendant's Response to Plaintiff's Request for Production of Documents on the following party by way of U.S. Mail.

E. Manning, Esq
Collection Agency
123 W 10th St.
Fairbanks, AK 99709

_____   _____
Date   Signature

The last part of the plaintiff's discovery is the request for admissions. If the plaintiff doesn't have any evidence to prove their case, they will try to make you prove their case for them. So if the contract is gone, but you say the debt is legit, then they can prove their case without the contract. Watch out for tricky questions. Remember, admit to nothing except name and address. You can use similar objections for all parts of the plaintiff's discovery. The main thing to remember is that you object to the plaintiff's request for (production of documents, interrogatories, or admissions) on the grounds that it is: vague, overbroad and unduly burdensome, or that it seeks to obtain information not within your possession, custody or control of defendant, or that the defendant has not been presented with any documentation in writing to bear out the truth of the plaintiff's claim, etc. There are hundreds of answers to the plaintiff's request for admissions available online. Do a Google search for "plaintiff request for admission debt" to view more examples.

DISTRICT COURT FOR THE STATE OF ALASKA

Collection Agency,	)	Case No.: 1234567
Plaintiff,	)	
vs.	)	
Joe Smith,	)	
Defendant	)	Defendant's Response to Plaintiff's Request for
	)	Admissions
	)	
	)	
	)	
	)	

Pursuant to The Federal Rules of Civil Procedure, the Defendant hereby responds to the Plaintiff's Request for Admissions as follows.

Admission #1: Please admit that you have a credit card account with AA Credit Cards.

Response: Defendant objects to this Request on the grounds that after reasonable inquiry the information known or readily obtainable by him is insufficient to accurately respond to this request. Plaintiff's complaint is utterly devoid of any factual information regarding the alleged debt and any agreement giving rise to the alleged debt.

Admission #2: Please admit that the debt amount listed in the Complaint is valid.

Response: Defendant objects to this Request on the grounds that it calls for a legal conclusion. Liability for debts alleged in a civil action are to be decided by the trier of fact, not the defendant.

Request #3: Please admit that the Defendant made monthly payments to AA Credit Cards.

Response: Defendant objects to this Request on the grounds that the Defendant has not been presented with any documentation in writing to bear out the truth of the Plaintiff's claim.

Request #4: Please admit that the Defendant's cardholder agreement with AA Credit Cards allows the recovery of collection fees and attorney fees.

Response: Defendant objects to this Request on the grounds that the Defendant has not been presented with any documentation in writing to bear out the truth of the Plaintiff's claim.

Request #5: Please admit that you did not dispute any of the fees and charges that were applied to the Defendant's account with AA Credit Cards.

Response: Defendant objects to this Request on the grounds that the Defendant has not been presented with any documentation in writing to bear out the truth of the Plaintiff's claim.

Request #6: Please admit that the Plaintiff has applied all just and lawful offsets to the account.

Response: Defendant objects to this Request on the grounds that the Defendant has insufficient information to affirm or deny and leaves to Plaintiff to provide proof.

Request #6: Please admit that AA Credit Cards offered a settlement to the Defendant.

Response: Defendant objects to this Request on the grounds that the Defendant has not been presented with any documentation in writing to bear out the truth of the Plaintiff's claim. Plaintiff should have records or documents of any settlements made to Defendant from Plaintiff's own files.

CERTIFICATE OF SERVICE

I, Joe Smith, hereby certify that on March 1, 2012, I served copies of the Defendant's Response to Plaintiff's Request for Admissions on the following party by way of U.S. Mail.

E. Manning, Esq
Collection Agency
123 W 10th St.
Fairbanks, AK 99709

_____   _____
Date   Signature

Once you receive the plaintiff's answers to your discovery, you will find out that they have truthfully answered little to nothing. Or sometimes they don't even mail out a response at all. The solution is very simple. File a motion to compel with the court. If you can get the judge to force them to answer, the plaintiff will probably lose their case. On the other hand, if they still refuse to answer, you can file a motion for summary judgment. This is usually when the plaintiff will request a voluntary dismissal without prejudice, so they have the option to sue you again if desired, or sell the debt to someone else.

As soon as you receive the plaintiff's response to your discovery, or on the day it is due, send a letter to the plaintiff's counsel asking them to answer your discovery request. Many states require that you in good faith try to solve the discovery dispute outside the courtroom. Remember to request a signature when shipping that out. You will need proof of delivery and a copy of the letter for your motion to compel. Below is a sample letter reminding the plaintiff to properly answer your discovery.

April 2, 2012

Joe Smith
Address
City, State, Zip

Dear Collection Agency:

This letter is a reminder that the Plaintiff's counsel was served with Interrogatories, a Request for Production of Documents, and a Request for Admissions on March 1, 2012. The Plaintiff's responses to same were due on April 1, 2012. To date, you have failed to comply with the demands for discovery by providing answers that were incomplete and evasive. Demand is hereby made for you to comply with the discovery requested within five (10) days of the date of this correspondence. Enclosed you will find a copy of the requested discovery. If you should have any questions, please contact me.

Sincerely,
Joe|Smith

When the plaintiff refuses your letter request, you can file a motion to compel. Be sure to check with your state and local court rules when filing any motion. You don't want the motion denied due to a technicality. Do a Google search for "(your state here) motion to compel" and see what comes up. After you file the motion to compel, find out from the clerk whether there will be a hearing set for this motion. If the judge does not need any additional information, he can decide on the motion without a hearing. If there is a hearing set, the clerk can give you a generic form to send to the plaintiff to notify them of the time and date. Often, if you have not received discovery responses by this point, the plaintiff probably never intended to actually fight the case. They were just looking for an easy default judgment. When you think about it, why should a collection agency even bother fighting 10% of their cases, when the other 90% are won with hardly any work at all?

Below is the motion to compel.

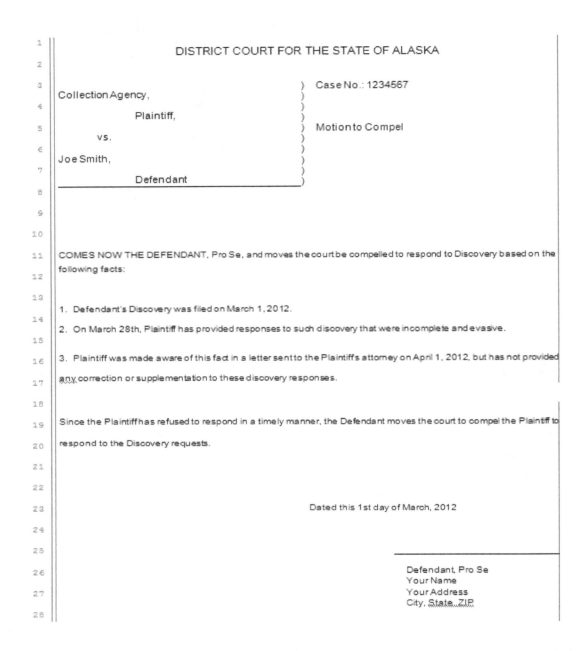

DISTRICT COURT FOR THE STATE OF ALASKA

Collection Agency,   )   Case No.: 1234567
)
                    Plaintiff,   )
)   Motion to Compel
        vs.   )
)
Joe Smith,   )
)
                    Defendant   )

COMES NOW THE DEFENDANT, Pro Se, and moves the court be compelled to respond to Discovery based on the following facts:

1. Defendant's Discovery was filed on March 1, 2012.

2. On March 28th, Plaintiff has provided responses to such discovery that were incomplete and evasive.

3. Plaintiff was made aware of this fact in a letter sent to the Plaintiff's attorney on April 1, 2012, but has not provided any correction or supplementation to these discovery responses.

Since the Plaintiff has refused to respond in a timely manner, the Defendant moves the court to compel the Plaintiff to respond to the Discovery requests.

Dated this 1st day of March, 2012

_____
Defendant, Pro Se
Your Name
Your Address
City, State, ZIP

Note: if you are ever losing your case, don't be afraid to change your course of action a bit and attack the numbers, logos, and seals. Did the plaintiff send you a copy of the correct membership agreement, or did they charge incorrect interest or fees? Were the official logos and seals located on the plaintiff's evidence (billing statements, affidavits, notary forms)? Was there an error in their computations somewhere? Find a number that is wrong in the complaint and dispute it. Make them account for every cent. Or you can always file a "motion to compel arbitration" to move the case to a more expensive venue for the plaintiff. Check your card member agreement and your state's rules for "alternative dispute resolution." Often, once you request arbitration, the trial date is removed and an arbitration hearing is scheduled if the plaintiff pays his fees. Look online for a copy of the cardmember agreement around the time of the alleged default.

DISTRICT COURT FOR THE STATE OF ALASKA

Collection Agency,	) Case No.: 1234567
Plaintiff,	)
vs.	)
Joe Smith,	)
Defendant	) Motion to Compel Arbitration
	)
	)
	)
	)
_____	)

COMES NOW THE DEFENDANT, Pro Se, to compel arbitration pursuant to the arbitration terms contained within the attached AA Credit Cards Cardmember Agreement.

1. The parties are bound by the Credit Card Agreement. The Arbitration Agreement states among other things:

(a) ARBITRATION –IT PROVIDES THAT ANY DISPUTE MAY BE RESOLVED BY BINDING ARBITRATION. ARBITRATION REPLACES THE RIGHT TO GO TO COURT, INCLUDING THE RIGHT TO A JURY AND THE RIGHT TO PARTICIPATE IN A CLASS ACTION OR SIMILAR PROCEEDING.

(b) IF YOU OR WE ELECT PRIVATE ARBITRATION OF A CLAIM, NEITHER YOU NOR WE WILL HAVE THE RIGHT TO PURSUE THAT CLAIM IN COURT OR BEFORE A JUDGE OR JURY.

2. The Supreme Court Ruling, AT&T MOBILITY LLC v. CONCEPCION ET U (2011), states that courts must enforce arbitration agreements according to their terms. If there is an arbitration clause in the contract, that clause must be honored.

WHEREFORE, the Defendant pray the Court grant the following;
1. That the Plaintiffs be compelled into arbitration per their agreement.
2. That the Plaintiff be compelled to initiate arbitration.
4. That this case be dismissed with prejudice.

CERTIFICATE OF SERVICE

I, Joe Smith, hereby certify that on May 1, 2012, I served copies of the Motion to Compel Arbitration on the following party by way of U.S. Mail.

E. Manning, Esq
Collection Agency
123 W 10th St.
Fairbanks, AK 99709

_____
Date

_____
Signature

Note: if the plaintiff files a motion for summary judgment before you do, you will need to file an opposition to the plaintiff's motion for summary judgment. The judge can then request a hearing, grant the motion, or deny the motion. Check out the example below. It basically says that the plaintiff has not proven that they are entitled to a legal remedy, and that there are still issues of material fact that are in dispute. In other words, you need to attack everything the plaintiff asserts in his motion for summary judgment. The lack of a contract and credible affidavit of debt are being attacked in this opposition to summary judgment example.

DISTRICT COURT FOR THE STATE OF ALASKA

Collection Agency,

         Plaintiff,

   vs.

Joe Smith,

        Defendant

) Case No.: 1234567
)
)
)
)
)
) Opposition to Plaintiff's Motion for Summary
) Judgment
)
)
)
)

COMES NOW THE DEFENDANT, Pro Se, and files this reply to the Plaintiff's Motion for Summary Judgment as follows:

1. Defendant received the Plaintiff's Summons on February 20, 2012. Defendant answered the request on March 1, 2012.

2. Trial was set for June 10th, 2012.

3. Defendant's Discovery was filed on March 1st, 2012.

4. Documents requested from Plaintiff included documentation of relationship between Plaintiff and AA Credit Cards, payment history, and a breakdown of the sum requested by Plaintiff.

4. The Plaintiff failed to properly respond to Defendant's Discovery requests which were sent via US Priority Mail. (Copy Attached). The Plaintiff's answers were incomplete and evasive.

5. The Plaintiff has failed to provide a contract, an agreement bearing the signature of the Defendant, or itemized statements or billing which would constitute intimate knowledge of the creation of the debt. **Advantage Physical Therapy Inc. v. Cruse 165 S.W.3d 21 (2005)**

6. Plaintiff's Affidavit is hearsay and presumes facts not in evidence. In face of answer denying all allegations of the complaint, an affidavit containing statement by officer of plaintiff that the allegations of the complaint were true is insufficient to support motion for summary judgment. **Nour v. All State Pipe Supply Co. 487 So.2d 1204 (1986)**

1 7. Summary judgment should not be granted unless the facts are so crystallized that nothing remains but questions

2 of law.   Spears v. Albertson's Inc. 848 So.2d 1176 (2003)

3

4 WHEREFORE, Defendant respectfully submits that the Court should deny the Plaintiff's Motion for Summary

5 Judgment

6

7

8

                                                    Dated this 1st day of May, 2012

9

10

11   _____

12   Defendant, Pro Se
                                                Your Name
                                                Your Address
13   City, State, ZIP

14

15

16

17

18

19

20   CERTIFICATE OF SERVICE

21 I, Joe Smith, hereby certify that on April 10, 2012, I served copies of the Opposition to the Plaintiff's Motion for
22 Summary Judgment on the following party by way of U.S. Mail.

23 E. Manning, Esq
24 Collection Agency
25 123 W 10th St.
26 Fairbanks, AK 99709

27 _____   _____
28 Date   Signature

An affidavit might need to be included with your opposition to summary judgment. Check your local court rules and find out when affidavits are required. An affidavit is a formal sworn statement of fact, signed by the declarant (who is also called the *affiant* or *deponent*) and witnessed (as to the veracity of the affiant's signature) by a notary public.

DISTRICT COURT FOR THE STATE OF ALASKA

Collection Agency,

    Plaintiff,

  vs.

Joe Smith,

    Defendant

)
)
)
)
)
)
)
)
)
)
)
)

Case No.: 1234567

Affidavit in Support of Opposition to Plaintiff's Motion for Summary Judgment

I, Joe Smith, herein after Defendant, being duly sworn, depose and declare that the statements made therein, are true and correct to the best of my knowledge, and not meant to mislead.

1. Defendant specifically denies that Plaintiff holds in due course any claim against the Defendant pursuant to an alleged credit card account as represented by an original credit agreement signed by the Defendant and held by the Plaintiff that is the subject of this dispute, and demands strict proof of the same by producing the original, unaltered alleged instrument for inspection by the Defendant and by the Court.

2. The validity of the records on which Plaintiff's affirmations of purchases and transactions made by the Defendant showing the balance allegedly due and owing was originally based is specifically denied.

Subscribed and sworn to before me this 4th day of May, 2012.

             _____

             Defendant, Pro Se
             Your Name
             Your Address
             City, State, ZIP

_____
Notary Public for Alaska
My commission expires
____ Day of _____, 2____.

CERTIFICATE OF SERVICE

I, Joe Smith, hereby certify that on May 4, 2012, I served copies of the Affidavit in Support of Opposition to Plaintiff's Motion for Summary Judgment on the following party by way of U.S. Mail.

E. Manning, Esq

Collection Agency

123 W 10th St.

Fairbanks, AK 99709

_____   _____

Date   Signature

Now it's time to send the debt collector packing . If you still have not received truthful discovery responses from the plaintiff, then it is time to file a motion for summary judgment. Here is the theory. If there is not enough admissible evidence to dispute the facts, or the facts are not in dispute at all, the judge will be able to apply law to the facts, and grant the summary judgment to the movant. That's the moving party. There is a heavy burden on the movant when it comes to summary judgment motions. Each claim has to be proven with case law. The opposing side has to disprove only one of those claims.

The example I have provided is a very basic motion. It has three parts: the material facts (facts that are the important ones), the legal argument, and conclusion. Here is how it works. You need to find case rulings that explain why you should win the case. One of the cases I have cited is very simple **(ADVANTAGE PHYSICALTHERAPY INC v. CRUSE)**. Breach of contract can't be granted without the contract being present. That's why businesses don't or shouldn't throw away contracts.

You can read about this case and others here:

http://caselaw.findlaw.com/tx-court-of-appeals/1303528.html

 Normally, when it comes to debt collection, we are looking for at least two contracts: one between the defendant and original creditor that established the debt, and one between the plaintiff and original creditor that established the right to collect the debt. However, when you get right down to it, there are many more contracts and addendums that are added to the original contract, since credit card agreements can be changed or amended at any time. In other words, the contract is continually being renewed and changed. You could argue that 20 or more contracts are needed to calculate a debt instead of just one. And there are even more contract issues that are troublesome for the debt buyers out there. If someone else purchased the debt before the plaintiff, then copies of those contracts need to be presented to the court as well. If the plaintiff can't show a complete chain of custody, then they can't prove they legally own the debt, or can ask the court for legal remedy. This becomes an even more critical issue with older debts. Debts can be bought and sold a dozen times, making it virtually impossible for any collector to prove chain of custody.

The other item to focus on is the affidavit of debt. If it hasn't been stricken by this point you are probably getting sued by an original creditor. But the affidavit still needs to be attacked before the bench trial. Destroy the credibility of the affiant and the information on the affidavit. Even if he has been with the company for 20 years, he still may just be robo-signing affidavits. Is your name and account number on the affidavit? Does the affiant provide any proof of what he is saying is correct? Were sworn or certified copies of documents provided with the affidavit? Include case law which states that affidavits are nothing more than hearsay. Also include your local court rule definition of "hearsay."

Below are some more case law examples that you can use in your motions or discovery. Try to find case law from your state court if possible and write it down for later use. Your state law will hold more weight with your local court. However, you can use case law from another state if needed. And the case does not even have to be about credit card debt to be useful. When you read over the cases, also look for citations to other cases that can help strengthen your arguments in court. Here are some examples of cases that may be of use.

RIZKALLAH v. CONNER - Conclusory statements in affidavits are not competent evidence to support a summary judgment.

Williams v. Unifund CCR Partners, Tully v. Citibank, Bird v. First Deposit Nat'l Bank, McCamant v. Batsell - Sworn account cannot be used as a claim because no title to personal property passes from the bank to the cardholder; rather, the card evidences a line of credit extended by the bank which the cardholder may use to purchase goods and services from a third party.

H & H Design Builders, Inc. v. Travelers' Indem - An itemized copy of the account must be attached to the complaint to state a valid claim; a statement of a lump sum balance due is insufficient.

Munoz v. Pipestone Financial, LLC - The plaintiff cannot collect interest and attorney fees, only the original creditor can.

Cherokee Oil Co. v. Union Oil Co. of California - One party cannot unilaterally create a liability on an open account when no contract (either oral or written) exists out of which a debtor-creditor relationship could arise.

Dionne v. Columbus Mills, Inc - Complaint failed to state cause of action for account stated where allegations therein did not show existence of a mutual agreement.

Page Avjet Corp. v. Cosgrove Aircraft Sers. - Failure to respond to demand for payment does not create obligation for account stated absent contractual agreement creating such liability.

You can download all of the court document examples here:

www.snotboards.com/court.zip

DISTRICT COURT FOR THE STATE OF ALASKA

Collection Agency,

           Plaintiff,

      vs.

Joe Smith,

           Defendant

Case No.: 1234567

Motion for Summary Judgment

COMES NOW THE DEFENDANT, Pro Se, and files this Motion for Summary Judgment as follows:

Statement of Material Facts

1. There is no admissible evidence regarding an alleged breach of contract by the Defendant. The Plaintiff has failed to provide a contract, an agreement bearing the signature of the Defendant, or itemized statements or billing which would constitute intimate knowledge of the creation of the debt.

2. Plaintiff's Affidavit is hearsay and presumes facts not in evidence.

Legal Arguments

1. Plaintiff has failed to prove its case under the theory of breach of contract. A credit card agreement cannot be enforced without evidence that it was actually offered. In order to prevail on a breach of contract claim, a plaintiff must prove the existence of a clearly defined contract between all parties. (ADVANTAGE PHYSICAL THERAPY INC v. CRUSE) (Wright v. Christian & Smith)

2. The Plaintiff has failed to provide a contract, an agreement bearing the signature of the Defendant, or itemized statements or billing which would constitute intimate knowledge of the creation of the debt. **Advantage Physical Therapy Inc. v. Cruse 165 S.W.3d 21 (2005)**

3. In face of answer denying all allegations of the complaint, an affidavit containing statement by officer of plaintiff that the allegations of the complaint were true is insufficient to support motion for summary judgment. **Nour v. All State Pipe Supply Co. 487 So.2d 1204 (1986)**

4. Statements contained in affidavits, to be considered on motion for summary judgment, must be of such evidentiary value that they would be admissible at trial. Garwood v. Equitable Life Insurance Society of U.S *299 So.2d 163 (1974)*

5. There is no documentation to substantiate the facts alleged or the derivation of the balance due. There are no bills, statements or receipts evidencing defendant's payment history, or the fees and expenses allegedly incurred. Bank of America, N.A. v Danniel Paggy 601802/09 (2011)

Conclusion

WHEREFORE, Defendant respectfully submits that the Court should grand the Defendant's Motion for Summary Judgment.

Dated this 10th day of May, 2012

_____

Defendant, Pro Se
Your Name
Your Address
City, State, ZIP

CERTIFICATE OF SERVICE

I, Joe Smith, hereby certify that on May 10, 2012, I served copies of the Defendant's Motion for Summary Judgment on the following party by way of U.S. Mail.

E. Manning, Esq
Collection Agency
123 W 10th St.
Fairbanks, AK 99709

_____   _____
Date   Signature

Here is the affidavit in support of your summary judgment. It states under oath that you do not owe the debt, so the case should be dismissed. Be sure to sign it in front of a notary before you take it to the court and mail it to the plaintiff.

DISTRICT COURT FOR THE STATE OF ALASKA

Collection Agency,	) Case No.: 1234567
Plaintiff,	)
vs.	) Affidavit in Support of Defendant's Motion for Summary Judgment
Joe Smith,	)
Defendant	)

I, Joe Smith, herein after Defendant, being duly sworn, depose and declare that the statements made therein, are true and correct to the best of my knowledge, and not meant to mislead.

1. Defendant specifically denies that Plaintiff holds in due course any claim against the Defendant pursuant to an alleged credit card account as represented by an original credit agreement signed by the Defendant and held by the Plaintiff that is the subject of this dispute, and demands strict proof of the same by producing the original, unaltered alleged instrument for inspection by the Defendant and by the Court.

2. The validity of the records on which Plaintiff's affirmations of purchases and transactions made by the Defendant showing the balance allegedly due and owing was originally based is specifically denied.

Subscribed and sworn to before me this 4th day of May, 2012.

_____
Defendant, Pro Se
Your Name
Your Address
City, State, ZIP

_____
Notary Public for Alaska
My commission expires
___ Day of _____, 2___.

2

3

4

5

6

7

8

9

10

11

12

13

14

CERTIFICATE OF SERVICE

I, Joe Smith, hereby certify that on May 4, 2012, I served copies of the Affidavit in Support of Defendant's Motion for Summary Judgment on the following party by way of U.S. Mail.

E. Manning, Esq

Collection Agency

123 W 10ᵗʰ St.

Fairbanks, AK 99709

_____   _____
Date   Signature

Note: keep in mind the sample case and forms mentioned in this book provide a roadmap for navigating around a basic and predictable debt collection lawsuit. There are many more strategies and techniques that can come into play which have not been discussed here. In any event, you can always use Google and the other resources mentioned in this book to find the pleadings and case law you need. Someone somewhere has written about a similar debt collection case that can help you out. Hopefully, you now have a better understanding of how debt collection litigation works. It's really not as scary as you thought. Plus, many of you reading this book will never be sued, never step in a courtroom, and never have to pay back your alleged debts. The statute of limitations will just run out. Just remember, you have nothing to lose by fighting. Even if you do lose, you have at least stopped the outrageous interest and fees from accumulating year after year. And there is always an appeals process, which can also be navigated through. In the long haul, you are saving money, and best of all, getting out of the debt slavery nightmare for good!

You can download all of the court document examples here:

www.snotboards.com/court.zip

STEP 5 – CHECKING YOUR CREDIT REPORT

A "credit report" is a tool financial institutions use to determine if you are creditworthy or not. However, checking your credit report involves a whole lot more than just seeing if you can get a loan. It can tell you who is running your credit report, who is doing soft or hard pulls, and who is potentially thinking about suing you. Your credit report tells the bill collectors everything they need to know in order to determine whether you are judgment proof or not: it tells them what credit cards you have, what loans you have, what payments you have made, what payments you have not made, your job title, where you live, and your social security number. If you have money to pay your credit bills, then they will find out. That is why you want to stop paying all of your credit cards at the same time.

On the other hand, the debt collectors are not the only ones to benefit from viewing a credit report. You can also obtain some useful information from your report. Specifically, you can find out who has been assigned to collect your debt, and who has purchased your debt. These are very important pieces of information. Odds are, the junk debt buyers are more likely to bring charges against you since they sue hundreds of thousands of people each year. So you need to take them seriously and prepare for a fight.

What makes you more likely to be sued by a debt collector? This is a very common question, but there really is no rule set in stone, since some bottom feeding collectors will sue just about anyone for any amount. There are a few things, however, that can increase your risk of being sued: not requesting debt validation, owing more than $1000, having a debt older than 12 months, making payments on other debts, and having your debt purchased by one of the sleazier collection agencies.

Attorney General Lori Swanson posted on her website some of the statistics involving Midland Funding, one of the nation's largest debt buyers. In 2009, they purchased over $54 billion in bad debt for pennies on the dollar, and filed 245,000 lawsuits. These purchases are financed by some of the biggest and powerful banks in the country, the ones protected by the politicians. If debt buyers are going to pump out lawsuits, they need robo-signers. Some of Midland's employees under sworn testimony admitted to signing up to 400 affidavits of debt per day, often not even looking at them. When 10% or less actually fight back, it's easy to see how the debt collectors can make ridiculous amounts of money without having to gather much legal evidence. You have to assume these scumbags will try to take you to court, too.

http://www.ag.state.mn.us/consumer/pressrelease/110328debtbuyers.asp

Let's look at your free credit report. You can view your report once per year at the site, www.annualcreditreport.com. This is a good place to start and is recommended by the FTC (http://www.ftc.gov/bcp/edu/pubs/consumer/credit/cre34.shtm). Be wary of other "free" credit reporting sites as they might not actually be free after the first 30 days. Annual Credit Report will give you three free credit reports: Equifax, Experian, and Trans Union. You can purchase additional credit reports in the future for under $10.

Once you are able to view your credit report, search for junk debt buyers. Once you find their name, it's time to do some research. You need to find case law that you can use to fight them in court if needed. Write down the cases that relate to potential affirmative defences that you may need to use. Search online for court cases with the junk debt buyer's name in the pleadings. You need to learn about the cases they won and lost. And if they lost, why? Are they pumping out bogus affidavits that are not even notarized? Or do they submit lists of transactions to the court which are not authenticated? Also, are they filing a sizeable number of lawsuits in your state? Don't wait. Start building your case now. Be sure to check out all of the top debt collection forums including this one:

http://www.collectorsexposed.com/forum/

Below is an example of a credit card company that sold or assigned the debt to a collection agency. Notice the activity is described as "transfer/sold."

P.O.Box 15298
Wilmington , DE-19850
(800) 955-9900

Account Number:		Current Status:	CHARGE-OFF
Account Owner:	Individual Account.	High Credit:	$ 2,229
Type of Account :	Revolving	Credit Limit:	$ 2,000

Term Duration:		Terms Frequency:	Monthly (due every month)
Date Opened:	03/2002	Balance:	$ 0
Date Reported:	04/2011	Amount Past Due:	
Date of Last Payment:	02/2011	Actual Payment Amount:	
Scheduled Payment Amount:	$ 1,154	Date of Last Activity:	N/A
Date Major Delinquency First Reported:	04/2011	Months Reviewed:	99
Creditor Classification:		Activity Description:	Transfer/Sold
Charge Off Amount:		Deferred Payment Start Date:	
Balloon Payment Amount:		Balloon Payment Date:	
Date Closed:		Type of Loan:	Credit Card
Date of First Delinquency:	07/2010		
Comments:	Charged off account		

Here is the payment history. The payments in red and orange are late. Green is on time.

81-Month Payment History

Year	Jan	Feb	Mar	Apr	May	Jun	Jul	Aug	Sep	Oct	Nov	Dec
2011	150	150	180									
2010	*	*	*	*	*	*	*	30	60	60	90	120
2009	*	*	*	*	*	*	*	*	*	*	*	*
2008	*	*	*	*	*	*	*	*	*	*	*	*
2007	*	*	*	*	*	*	30	*	*	*	*	*
2006	*	*	*	*	*	*	*	*	*	*	*	*
2005	*	*	*	*	*	*	*	*	*	*	*	*
2004							*	*	*	*	*	*

	09/1999	$0	03/2011	CHARGE-OFF $3,349

Below is an example of a collection agency that purchased an alleged debt.

EQUABLE ASCENT FINANCIAL, LLC

1120 W LAKE COOK RD
SUITE B
BUFFALO GROVE , IL-60089-1970
(866) 902-7395

Account Number:	XXX	Current Status:	
Account Owner:	Individual Account.	High Credit:	$ 1,806
Type of Account :	Open	Credit Limit:	
Term Duration:		Terms Frequency:	
Date Opened:	04/2011	Balance:	$ 1,806
Date Reported:	01/2012	Amount Past Due:	$ 1,806
Date of Last Payment:		Actual Payment Amount:	
Scheduled Payment Amount:		Date of Last Activity:	N/A
Date Major Delinquency First Reported:	06/2011	Months Reviewed:	7
Creditor Classification:		Activity Description:	N/A
Charge Off Amount:		Deferred Payment Start Date:	
Balloon Payment Amount:		Balloon Payment Date:	
Date Closed:		Type of Loan:	Factoring Company Account (debt buyer)
Date of First Delinquency:	07/2010		
Comments:	Collection account		

Here is a list of companies that ran the credit report. These are soft pulls so they don't hurt your credit score. Notice the credit cards and collection agencies on the list. They are looking for money!

Inquiries that do not impact your credit rating

These inquires include requests from employers, companies making promotional offers and your own requests to check your credit. These inquiries are only viewable by you.

Company Information	Date of Inquiry
PRM-AMORED INVESTMENT GROUP	03/02/11
PRM-AT&T WIRELESS	01/27/12, 10/26/11
PRM-BANK OF ENGLAND	11/14/11
AR-CAPITAL ONE	10/04/11
AR-CITI CARDS CBNA	12/30/11
EQUIFAX	02/02/12, 04/05/11, 02/27/11
ND-EQUIFAX	12/12/10
FAIR ISAAC	02/27/11
AR-HSBC BANK NEVADA	05/17/11
AR-HOUSEHOLD BANK	03/17/11
AR-LN- PHILLIPS AND COHENASSOC.	08/12/11
PRM-YORK REGION COLLECTION SERV	04/13/11

Here is a collection agency that has been assigned one of the debts.

Collections

A collection is an account that has been turned over to a collection agency by one of your creditors because they believe the account has not been paid as agreed.

CAVALRY PORTFOLIO SERVICES	
Agency Address:	500 SUMMIT LAKE DRIVE VALHALLA, NY 10595 (800) 501-0909
Date Reported:	12/2011
Date Assigned:	04/2011
Creditor Classification:	Banking
Creditor Name:	███████████████████
Accounts Number:	██████████
Account Owner:	Individual Account.
Original Amount Owned:	$707
Date of 1 st Delinquency:	07/2010
Balance Date:	12/2011
Balance Owned:	$731
Last Payment Date :	N/A
Status Date:	12/2011
Status:	D - Unpaid
Comments:	Consumer disputes this account information

Instructions for disputing your credit report.

Frequently Asked Questions

How can I dispute inaccuracies on my CSC CREDIT SERVICES credit file?

As stated in the FCRA, you have the right to dispute information that you feel is being reported incorrectly on your credit file. You are able to initiate an online investigation immediately or you can contact our dispute center at the toll-free number listed on your credit file.

To initiate an online investigation, click here Your investigation requests are covered by the FCRA.

Additionally, you can dispute inaccuracies via US mail by writing to:

Write to CSC CREDIT SERVICES at PO Box 619054, DALLAS, TX 75261-9054

How can I check the status of my dispute?

Click here to check the status of your investigation.

Please note: credit reporting company will notify you of the results of its investigation upon its completion. Investigations may take up to 30 days. Investigations because of your FACT Act free disclosure may take up to 45 days.

If the error has been fixed, you can have the credit reporting company send the corrected file to anyone who received the inaccurate file in the past six months (two years in the case of employers).

If you find an inaccuracy with one credit reporting agency, you may want to get your credit file from the other two agencies to see if their files contain the same error. After you've corrected an error with one agency, the other agencies should eventually receive the corrected information. But for prompt correction, it's best to contact each of the these agencies individually yourself:
Experian 1-888-397-3742
TransUnion 1-800-916-8800

When disputing your credit report, send each credit reporting agency (Equifax, Experian, Trans Union) a dispute letter each month. Be sure to use a different excuse each time, or else they will not conduct an investigation. Often, these agencies can't keep up with the demand to investigate each claim, so they will just remove the item from your report, which will improve your credit score. Below are some good example reasons you can use to dispute your credit report, which are published online at:
http://www.goodcreditco.com/howto-disputecreditscore.html

- Credit Record Not Mine
- Credit reported is wrong amount
- Item included is wrong account number
- Incorrect Charge-Off Date
- Credit item last Activity Date incorrect
- Credit reflects incorrect Balance
- Incorrect status reported
- Wrong High Credit Number
- Incorrect reporting of late pay month

Note: if you are disputing entries from collectors that might sue you, do not admit to owing the debt in your excuse. You can say the debt is not yours, or the account number is wrong. Don't say the balance is wrong, or else you admitted to owing the debt. If you end up in court and the plaintiff claims you never disputed the debt, that won't be the case. You can claim you did dispute the debt with the creditor and the credit reporting agency. The debt was not validated by the original creditor, so your only course of action was to dispute it with the reporting agency. Remember, credit card companies get purchased and change names all the time, so this is a legitimate concern for many people who don't recognize the company listed on the collection letter.

If you already settled the account with the creditor, disputing the report will be much easier since you have plenty of excuses to use. Check online for even more.

4/25/11

Name
Address
City, State, Zip

Re: Credit Report Dispute

Dear Equifax,

This letter is a formal request to correct inaccurate information contained in my credit file. The items listed below are inaccurate:

1. First Premier Account # 1234 5678 1234 5678
Requested Correction: This account has been paid in full. I am requesting that the item be removed to correct the information.

In accordance with the federal Fair Credit Reporting Act (FCRA), I respectfully request you investigate my claim and, if after your investigation, you find my claim to be valid and accurate, I request that you immediately delete the item. Thank you for your cooperation.

Sincerely,

Signature
Your Name

You can download this document here:

www.snotboards.com/equifaxletter.zip

ECONOMIC SOLUTIONS FOR EVERYONE

There are many ways that debtors and non-debtors alike can fight the fraudulent and abusive practices of the mega banks. I think everyone can agree that companies that fund dishonest collection agencies, commit mortgage backed security fraud, and hyper inflate the economy are bad for this country. And they do all of this after receiving billions in bailouts from your tax dollars! Something must be done on a large scale. It would be nice if we could round up the billionaire bankers that caused this mess and throw them in jail just like they did in Iceland, but it probably won't happen anytime soon. These scumbags are needed to fund the top tier candidates for both political parties. So let's look for a more realistic approach.

According to the website, **Move Your Money**, there is one thing you can do to take the power away from the big Wall Street mega Banks and transfer it to the local financial institutions. Close your savings and checking accounts and move them to a local community bank or credit union. In the end, you will probably get a lower interest rate and much better service.

But that is not all, you can also back politicians that are pushing for real banking reform. Support the ones that want to audit the Federal Reserve or reinstall the Glass-Steagall Act of 1932, so that banks can't use your money for risky investments, or give it away in secret bailouts. Become a volunteer in a political campaign, or start your own blog. Support alternative news sources that are engaged in exposing Wallstreet greed and corruption, or make your own youtube videos blasting those involved in exploiting the poor. Get involved, and let everyone know that they, too, can fight the big banks, collection agencies, and junk debt buyers in one form or another. With a little knowledge, we can prevent our brothers and sisters from falling victim to these greedy banksters. The famous American writer, Napoleon Hill, once said "Victory is always possible for the person who refuses to stop fighting." So keep on fighting! Good luck.

http://moveyourmoneyproject.org

The Move Your Money project is a nonprofit campaign that encourages individuals and institutions to divest from the nation's largest Wall Street banks and move to local financial institutions. Little has changed to prevent another financial crisis or to end 'Too Big To Fail,' and with Congress unwilling to act, we are encouraging individuals to take power into their own hands by voting with their dollars and no longer contributing to a financial system that has led our country astray. We are a campaign that gives people real, concrete actions they can take to create a more sane, stable and localized banking system.

Blog	Press	Why You Should Move Your Money?
"He has a right to speak" said the cop to the banker Guest Blog by marvinborg Like most bullies, the banks are cowards. They talk a big game, but if confronted with their...	Director of Move Your Money film Eugene Jarecki interviewed on Democracy Now! As participants in the Occupy Wall Street movement continue protesting the record profits made by banks bailed out by...	• INVEST IN MAIN STREET, NOT WALL STREET • END TOO BIG TO FAIL • FEWER FEES, MORE SAVINGS
Move Your Money on November 5th "Remember, Remember the 5th of November" On November 5th, also known as Guy Fawkes Day, hundreds, potentially thousands...	WVTM Covers Move Your Money Occupy Columbus will picket and stage a march near the Wells Fargo on 13th Street on Saturday. A press release sent to...	• GET MORE PERSONAL SERVICE • LEND A HAND TO LOCAL BUSINESSES

UPDATES

You can periodically check online for free updates to this book. New information will be posted here regarding original creditors, collection agencies, junk debt buyers, and litigation when and if it becomes available. So be sure to check this link after reading the book.

www.snotboards.com/creditupdates.html

You can send questions or comments to this address: info@snotboards.com

CPSIA information can be obtained
at www.ICGtesting.com
Printed in the USA
BVHW01s1324170718
521838BV00025B/193/P